Notes of Praise

"I was inspired by the insights in this book. Aggressive in style and worldly realistic, *The Executive Transition Playbook* is a reminder that business is built on relationships and makes a compelling case that to achieve results in a new role starts with choosing how to lead. This is a book for leaders who want to step up, lean in, and accelerate personal growth in their progressive and sequential career path. Well written, with exceptionally clear reasoning, *The Playbook* is a great read and a testament to why we should listen to Hilary Potts. It's a must-read for every executive coach, and for anyone who wants to lead as if they're being coached."

Thomas A. Kolditz, PhD
Brigadier General, US Army (ret.)
Professor Emeritus and former Head of Behavioral Sciences and Leadership, West Point
Professor and Director, Leader Development Program, Yale School of Management
Executive Director, Doerr Center for New Leaders, Rice University

"This book captures the essence of pragmatic leadership principles. Hilary Potts' book is a valuable learning tool for progressive leaders. Use it!"

Derrick Samuel, former President of Colgate Palmolive Company

"I have seen too many executives stumble when making a transition. Errors made in the critical first 100 days of a new leadership role can haunt you for a long time. Every executive and manager — as well as advisors to executives — should read *The Executive Transition Playbook*. It is an easy read and yet a comprehensive guide that should be a must-have on every leader's reading list."

Andrew Neitlich, Director, Center for Executive Coaching

"Hilary Potts shares clear and sensible tools to create a leadership transition plan designed to maximize your success in a new role. *The Executive Transition Playbook* is essential for leaders looking to build a strategy for both quick impact and long-term success."

Kristen Clendaniel Clark, consumer package goods industry executive

"Hilary Potts has been a coach, friend, and partner through many leader transitions. I found the *Playbook* very helpful in identifying both where I succeeded and where I could do better. It's great to have it now fully developed and written down in an easy-to-follow manner. Thanks, Hilary!"

Andrew Towle, Managing Director, Kellogg
Australia and New Zealand

"In working with Boards, I've seen a number of executives who, when joining a new firm, become overwhelmed and unintentionally get off track. *The Executive Transition Playbook* offers executives simple strategies to help them regain their focus and achieve solid results."

Nancy May, President and CEO, The BoardBench Companies

"This is an excellent book that I encourage all executives in transition to read…the holy grail for effective leadership transitions."

Jayne Warrilow, CEO, Resonant Coaching

"Hilary Potts has been a trusted advisor of mine for years. Her formula for executives entering new roles is compelling and practical, and echoes Hilary's personal passion and wisdom for helping leaders successfully transform businesses."

Robert E. Maher, CEO & Board Advisor;
former CEO of New York Cruise Line

"A terrific read for any leader who wants to accelerate their success in a new role. This book captures a wealth of proven experience and wisdom to help the reader discover their own path to leadership success. *The Executive Transition Playbook* is chock-full of practical, actionable advice that is guaranteed to expand your thinking. I found myself reflecting on many of the insights long after I finished reading it."

David O'Brien, President, WorkChoice Solutions
Best-selling author of *The Navigator's Handbook; 101 Leadership Lessons for Work and Life;* and *The Navigator's Compass: 101 Steps Toward Leadership Excellence*

"*The Executive Transition Playbook* offers principles and practices for leaders to perform at their best within a short learning curve. The book fills a void in executive transition education. Ms. Potts' book is required reading for my clients as they transition into new roles!"

Linda M. Van Valkenburgh, MS, CCMC, CJSS, CSMCS, CELDC
Founder, My Executive Career Coach

"It's not often I get to read a leadership transition book as useful as this. It contains well-thought-out, actionable content that is as easy to read as implement. Now it's up to executives to put the advice into practice."

Stuart Elliott, Founder, Double C Coaching

"*The Executive Transition Playbook* needs to be in the toolkit of every leader in transition. It is practical, effective, and immediately actionable. It will ensure executive success as it minimizes and removes much angst and possible derailment. A tremendous, must-have resource!"

Jasbindar Singh, business psychologist, leadership coach, author and speaker, Auckland, New Zealand

"No one knew that they wanted an iPhone until they actually saw the iPhone — what it enabled them to do, and how it helped their lives become more meaningful. That's essentially what Hilary Potts has done here. She has created the enabler that makes the life of an executive in transition have more meaning and achieve greater impact."

Vafa Akhavan, Founder and senior advisor, NueBridge

THE EXECUTIVE TRANSITION PLAYBOOK

Strategies for **Starting Strong**, **Staying Focused**, and **Succeeding** in Your New

ISBN-13: 978-1515360759

6075X

I dedicate this book to leaders who are passionate about making a difference every day. May you continue to learn and work on yourself, building and refining your skills, so that you may lead with the grace and wisdom of an authentic leader.

Contents

Illustrations

Introduction

Congratulations! You are moving into a new role in a new company or are taking on a new leadership role in your current company. You have come to the right place for support. A new role requires finding out how to be most effective at serving those people in the new environment, so that you all can achieve business results. *The Executive Transition Playbook* provides the information you need to streamline your transition period and quickly make a positive impact on the business.

The strategies, tips, and tools you will find in this book come from my more than three decades of experience as a business leader and advisor. As a change consultant and leadership strategist, I advise executives leading global enterprises on how best to make successful, rapid transitions into new roles. Additionally, I have experienced, first-hand, numerous business transitions and have seen countless transitions by my colleagues.

Over the years, I have noticed consistent themes in successful transitions and learned to be wary of potential traps experienced by transitioning leaders. In *The Executive Transition Playbook*, I share the insights I have gathered, to help you maximize your own transition activities. This *Playbook* provides a complete approach to creating a transition strategy, along with ample discussion of the tactical and interpersonal aspects of a transition. Leaders who have applied these principles were able to set up themselves *and* their organizations for success.

The reason for the creation of your own Executive Transition Playbook is to develop a strategy for your transition as well as to prepare you for the many conversations with colleagues, direct reports, and senior management that you will experience. *The Executive Transition*

Playbook outlines practical and simple techniques to create your transition plan in a format that you can easily access and use with others. It is a strategic thinking exercise and *not* about filling out the templates in a specific format. The tables and figures throughout this book are meant to act as visual guides for you as you devise your own transition plan.

Who Should Read This Book

The Executive Transition Playbook presents an approach that works for many executives. The information in the book will help senior leaders who are moving into new roles, whether those roles are in a different company, a promotion, or an expanded role in the current companies. The creation of an Executive Transition Playbook can be extremely helpful to executives in the midst of a restructuring or as part of merger integration activities. Often, the business takes precedence and the leader may not spend enough time assessing how their role affects the business.

I will talk to you directly, as if you are moving into a senior executive role. I will present a method to help you think through your transition and lay out plans that help you to quickly make valuable contributions to the business. Indeed, for those of you moving into any managerial or executive role, you will find the information in this book useful and on target to your transition. Leaders at all levels can benefit by using the *Playbook* as a guide when entering new roles.

How This Book Can Enhance Your Transition Effectiveness

Many leaders who have used *The Executive Transition Playbook* said they developed a clearer strategy and approach to their transition. They found a balance between cultivating relationships and gathering and assessing business information. These leaders felt better prepared and positioned to make a strategic contribution, because early on they spent time actively listening to and learning from others.

Leaders who created an Executive Transition Playbook of their own felt they had a better view of what their transition period would look like. They could devote more time to interacting with people, instead of feeling rushed moving from one thing to another, without the chance to take anything in. As a result, these leaders developed a better appreciation of the business and were able to make significant contributions to it early in their new role. Without a Playbook to guide them, these new leaders could easily have underestimated complexities, overlooked important items, and focused on entirely the wrong actions.

The most important factor in a successful transition is to take action. This requires a commitment to strengthening your own leadership and creating a strategy for your transition. This starts with establishing clear goals for your transition, so that you know what you need to achieve.

How to Use This Book

The Executive Transition Playbook presents structured steps to create your own Executive Transition Playbook. This book explains in detail the components of the Playbook, and tells you how to apply the concepts to your own situation. You already know how to lead businesses, so you just need a way to strategize and organize your approach to transition into a specific role.

I suggest that you read through the book first, to get a sense of this approach. It is a quick read. Then you can move to what interests you and focus on the material you need. The creation of your own Playbook is an iterative process, whether you work in chapter order or dive in wherever you want. Although simply reading through this material will help you, actually working with the information will show you how to make your transition process your own, so that you get what you need out of it. By the end of this process, you will have your strategy, plans, and actions aligned in a logical sequence that will be easy to implement.

Whenever I work with transitioning executives, I ask them to take at least 10 to 20 minutes per day to review their personal Playbook and to reflect on the activities they have gathered in it. The Playbook allows leaders to collect all their information in one place. It provides the structure and focus that enables leaders to develop key relationships and accelerate through the process, with far less stress.

An essential part of your transition is building accountability into the process. Some leaders work with a Human Resources professional or a trusted colleague, while others may turn to someone they respect outside the organization, such as a coach or consultant who is a transition expert. An outside coach or accountability partner can be an impartial, objective partner who will assist you in staying on top of what you need to do. A coach can help you assess the information and impressions you are gathering, so that you can develop effective plans for leading the organization. A coach can make sure you pay attention, cover all areas, and include all pertinent information in your Playbook.

Your Next Steps

The first step is to get started. This book is laid out in easy-to-use sections. Part I discusses the elements for a successful transition, from goal-setting to reviewing the Executive Transition Playbook. Chapter 1 helps you think through your transition readiness. The Executive Transition Playbook is introduced in Chapter 2. There you will also find more detailed templates and ideas for establishing your transition goals. It is important to write down your transition goals and get in the habit of moving them beyond ideas and concepts into action. Chapter 3 starts you thinking about how you will lay out your transition and the Executive Transition Playbook timeline of activities. Chapter 4 details typical ways in which transitions get derailed and simple steps to get yourself back on track.

Part II prepares you to lead in a new way, from learning about the business, to stepping confidently into the new role, to finding your personal balance and cadence. The chapters in Part III then walk you through preparing for the many conversations and meetings you will have with business colleagues and management, so that you can engage and communicate your ideas and new initiatives with confidence. Part IV presents suggestions that enable you to become more effective and proficient in leading in new ways as you move into your new role. An Executive Transition Sourcebook is introduced as a mechanism to gather and organize all the pertinent business information.

Finally, Part V positions you for long-term success. The chapters in this part present ways to assess and analyze the information. Once you organize it into key themes, you will be ready to share your observations with others. The next-to-last chapter, Chapter 25, walks you through how to take the information gathered in the transition and create a What's Next Plan to guide you over the next 6 to 18 months.

I wish you the best in your new role, and I hope my ideas and tools will help you transition successfully. If you find this book useful, please recommend it to others who are making transitions. For more information and ideas on leader transitions, you are always welcome to visit my website, **www.executivetransitionplaybook.com**. I would appreciate your comments.

May you have much success in making a smooth transition into your new role!

Hilary Potts
Middlebury, Connecticut

PART I

Assembling the Elements for a Successful Transition

Chapter 1

Taking Charge of Your Transition

There are no secrets to success. It is the result of preparation, hard work, and learning from failure.

– Colin Powell

Set Yourself Up for Success

Corporate boards, investors, and senior management alike all count on the talents and accomplishments of a new executive to guide their business forward. They visualize the contributions — in terms of revenue and earnings — that the new leader will deliver. They expect a fairy-tale story: With a wave of a magic wand, or so they think, associates are inspired, customers abound, and innovative solutions lead to expanding markets.

Unfortunately, the reality is that an estimated 40 percent of executives in new roles fail in the first two years. The cost of failure and lost productivity can add up to millions of dollars merely in recruiting expenses, signing bonuses, and compensation packages, in addition to the costs to the business. And you, the new executive, face the possibility of looking for another new role in less than two years.

Since you are reading this book, you are most likely looking for a better way to ensure your successful entry into a new role. You may want to make changes to effectively integrate into the business, but you aren't quite sure how to approach these changes. Maybe you have seen too many of your colleagues get tripped up in their transitions and do not want this to happen to you. Perhaps you realize that the transition plans you used in the past may not be adequate for this new role. Whatever the reason, I commend you for this awareness. The Executive Transition Playbook presented in this book will assist you in navigating your entry into a new role.

Often, executives spend all their time on what the business needs, and they run out of time for themselves. It's easy to assume you know how to transition, as you've probably changed roles many times throughout your career. Unfortunately, some leaders equate transition plans with onboarding and orientation checklists, instead of seeing a transition plan as a strategic planning tool.

The ideas in this book come from actual executive transitions. Not every issue will apply to your situation. Still, I truly care about helping you avoid common mistakes so you can successfully integrate into your new role.

I have seen far too many executives decide to forego a transition plan, assuming they could make a positive contribution without the plan. Sadly, these leaders find themselves 8 to 12 months into the new role struggling with business relationships or lacking the full understanding of the business that's needed for them to make strategic decisions. Many don't even realize that the lack of a transition plan is a key cause of their struggles. A tool such as the Executive Transition Playbook helps leaders create a strategy and a prioritized transition plan to avoid making any missteps when entering a new role.

At times, I may be stating the obvious. I have found that the simplest and most obvious leadership concepts are easily intellectualized, but harder to apply on a routine basis. Simple leadership fundamentals can be overlooked when more challenging issues present themselves.

Let's face it: Expectations are high, whether they come from the Board, the market, the new team, or senior management. Extraordinary leaders know their role is to serve the people and the business and to take the necessary actions to ensure that they are fully equipped to support others. Leaders are keen to get started, as they have quite a bit of ground to cover in a short time. You may prefer to pay attention to what interests you versus what's important and needs attention. Successful leaders know, though, that a transition is a time to thoroughly learn about and assess the new business.

When leaders incorporate simple leadership fundamentals into their transition plans, they are better equipped to navigate challenging situations. These leaders are prepared for the conversations that focus on building relationships and creating unique solutions.

The first few months are critical to getting established and making first impressions. To get the most out of your transition, go beyond seeing your transition as a one-off, three-month project and create a strategy and a plan to extend the themes of your transition into the next 6, 12, or 18 months. This allows you to move effectively from the "honeymoon" period to making a full contribution to the team. This requires having a way to quickly review and assess the business. It entails building the relationships and developing plans appropriate to the business situation. The Executive Transition Playbook is designed to do just that: to help you identify what you need to learn and to make plans to get up-to-speed. In Chapter 2, I present the Executive Transition Playbook and talk about its components.

First, though, take a look at yourself: Are you ready to make a successful transition? Are you prepared to handle the personal and interpersonal characteristics a transition requires?

Assess Your Transition Readiness

Before you develop and implement your transition plan, use the questions below to assess your transition readiness. In your analysis, consider the willingness of the organization to accept you in your new role. Figure 1-1 outlines questions to help you get ready for the transition.

As you answer these questions, you can see what you need to address to make your transition successful. The transition readiness assessment gives you a starting point to create your Executive Transition Playbook.

Transition Readiness Questions
Figure 1-1

1. **What are your transition goals?**
   - Why were you asked to take on this new role?
   - What does a successful transition into the new role look like?
   - What's most important to those who hired you?
   - Name three to five specific goals you want to accomplish in your transition into this new role.
   - Describe your leadership vision and objectives for this new assignment.
   - What potential obstacles might you encounter during your transition?

2. **How much do you know about the business?**
   - How would you describe the business as it stands today?
   - What have you been told about what is working and not working in the business?
   - What areas of the business have the most potential?
   - What preconceived notions do you have about the business, organization, processes, people, or culture?
   - What areas of the business concern you the most?

Figure 1-1 *continued*

3. How will your current leadership skills align with this new role?

- What are your leadership strengths, and how will they help you in the transition?

- Name your leadership vulnerabilities you need to be aware of as you come into this new position.

- How would you describe your personal leadership brand?

- What are your core values that help you lead effectively?

- What will you do to align your leadership approach with the company's culture and ways of working?

- How will you approach communications? What will you do to communicate with the right frequency and consistency?

- How will you honor your personal activities and obligations?

4. How will you make the right connections?

- Who are the key people you need to get to know?

- What will people want to know about you that will put them at ease?

- Whom can you count on and trust to help you through the transition?

- Is there anyone you would be uncomfortable meeting? What are your concerns?

5. What will people in that business say about you after your first few months in the role?

- What do people expect from you?

- How do you wish to be perceived by the Board, the shareholders, and the industry and markets you serve?

- What do you want your team to say about your leadership?

- What is your peer group saying about your leadership approach?

- What are people saying about how you are addressing the business challenges?

- How would people describe the impact you have had on the business?

Chapter 2

Understanding the Executive Transition Playbook

The secret of getting started is breaking your complex, overwhelming tasks into small manageable tasks, and then starting on the first one.

– Mark Twain

Don't Talk Yourself Out of a Transition Plan

You have transitioned so many times that you know the drill. You are busy with your new duties, and the business comes first. Things come up that need your immediate attention, so you decide to forego a transition plan. Maybe you plan to make leadership adjustments once you know the business needs and after you get settled. Taking time to create a plan may feel like it's cutting into valuable face time with colleagues and potential allies. However, if Benjamin Franklin were here he would say, "If you fail to plan, you are planning to fail."

Imagine a veteran pilot who says he doesn't need to review the flight plan because he's flown the same route so many times. In essence, executives who elect to work without their own transition plans are like pilots operating without flight plans. You might know what to do; however, each situation is a bit different. When an issue arises, as it does with every pilot, you will want to know how to respond.

Use your transition to create a strategy to test out assumptions and leadership approaches. When colleagues know you are actively engaged in your transition, it opens the door for others to share information and give you the feedback to keep your transition on track.

Many leaders confuse "onboarding," or orientation, programs with leader transitions. Onboarding and orientations help introduce a new employee to the company and cover logistics, training programs, policies, procedures, and other basics about the company.

Transition planning is more strategic and can shorten the learning curve to achieve success quickly, but not every organization offers such assistance in a formalized way. The Executive Transition Playbook provides a strategy for how to review the business and get engaged. The Playbook easily incorporates onboarding and orientation items. Ultimately, you will want to look at your transition more strategically to make sure it covers the key learning, communications, and social interactions you need to get up-to-speed.

The Executive Transition Playbook

The Executive Transition Playbook takes a strategic approach to prioritizing and sequencing a series of interactions, so that a new leader can move swiftly to take full responsibility for the business. Figure 2-1 presents the five steps in the Executive Transition Playbook: Set Goals, Develop the Transition Plan, Assess the Business, Share Observations, and Step into Action.

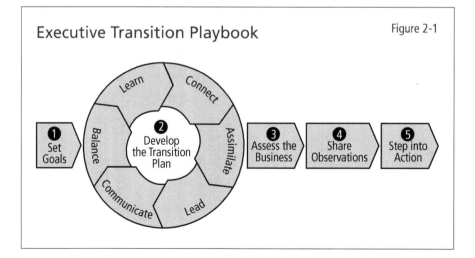

Executive Transition Playbook   Figure 2-1

The process starts with Setting Goals for the transition, ones that are aligned with what you and the organization want to accomplish in that transition. The next step is to create a Transition Plan using the six components — Learn, Connect, Assimilate, Lead, Communicate, and Balance. The remaining steps of the Executive Transition Playbook show you ways to Assess what you have learned, Share your information with your stakeholders, and Step into Action, as you help lead the organization forward.

One executive I worked with said the Playbook updated his own toolkit. He described the Playbook as a sophisticated, laserlike approach that enabled him to streamline his transition activities. The Executive Transition Playbook keeps you focused on what matters while you create the version of the Playbook that works for you in your particular transition.

Throughout the rest of this book, you will have an opportunity to explore each of the components of the Executive Transition Playbook.

Establish Your Transition Strategy and Goals

Goal setting is the first step to goal achieving.

It's surprising how many executives believe that merely taking on a new role is the goal itself. They celebrate the promotion or hiring and miss the opportunity to use the transition to create new leadership milestones. Then these executives quickly turn their attention from the promotion to the next goal: achieving the business's targets. But these executives bypass the critical interim process of assessing their entrance into the role and estimating the impact their leadership will have on future business performance. Without an Executive Transition Playbook, it can be difficult to measure how well the leader is truly serving the organization.

Being a servant leader means focusing on the growth and well-being of the people and the communities the leader serves. It's about taking care of the business by attending to others. When employees can perform at their best, the company thrives.

The Executive Transition Playbook gives the leader a preview to all aspects of the business so as to be of best service. You can create the work environment that achieves the desired results in the right way. The best way to start this process is through establishing clear goals for the transition. What is written down, gets done. Clear goals enable you to check your plans against what you want to accomplish, and against what the organization wants you to accomplish, to ensure that what you do makes a substantial contribution. At times, what others expect you to do and what you think is important may not be in sync. As the leader, your role is to find ways to ensure that there is clear goal alignment.

Figure 2-2 outlines Leader Transition Goals and Strategy as the first step in the Executive Transition Playbook. It has separate sections to capture the business goals versus your personal goals. By establishing both business and personal goals, you will be able to find ways to develop both the business and yourself.

It's a mistake to move from goal setting to action without first outlining a strategy and a set of plans to achieve your goals. Throughout the transition period, revisit your Leader Transition Goals and Strategy to stay on track.

Align Your Transition Strategy to the Business Situation

You need a strategy for determining the right way to approach a leader transition. Many leaders focus too much on what they want to do, and forget to consider the business environment and the people. What works in one situation could fail in another.

Leader Transition Goals and Strategy   Figure 2-2

Here is what I know about the business:

I would describe the current business situation as:

My business goals for this transition are:

My personal goals for this transition are:

Based on the business situation, my transition strategy is:

The following leadership principles will guide my transition:

Below is a list of the internal and external associates, groups, and organizations I would like to meet during my transition:

I will use the following strategy to develop relationships and connections with business colleagues:

Here is what colleagues will be saying about me after my first three months in the role:

I will know my transition was successful if...

Depending on the business, you may inherit a business strategy, or you may need to create a whole new strategy. Knowing the business situation gives you an indication of what you need to do. If the business is achieving its goals, you have the opportunity to listen and learn. In a turnaround situation, you may need to begin setting direction sooner. A start-up business could require a faster-paced transition to get things up-and-running. Knowing the situation will help you set your goals for the transition.

- Take a good look at the business today to determine its current situation.
- Is the business a high-growth start-up or a well-established business?
- Does the business need some major adjustments or just minor ones?
- Is it a mature business in a state of stagnation or decline that could use a boost in revenue growth?
- Is the company in the midst of a business transformation, or are key initiatives in progress?
- What other leadership changes are occurring at the same time as yours?

Understanding the business environment is critical in determining how you will lead through the transition and beyond. This may mean making adjustments to how you prefer to lead in favor of what the business requires. Remember, simply because the business could be in trouble doesn't mean you can forego a transition plan. In fact, this situation may require a more thoughtful transition strategy to ensure that your entry helps the performance of the business, instead of taking the business further off-track.

Determine the factors that led the Board, the owners, or the senior managers to make a change in the leadership at this time. Take a look at how the business situation will affect your interactions and decision-making in the first 30-, 60-, or 90-day period.

The Components of the Executive Transition Playbook

The second step in the Executive Transition Playbook is to create a transition plan using the six components: Learn, Lead, Connect, Assimilate, Communicate, and Balance. The Playbook is designed to provide both the structure and the flexibility to enable you to develop a customized transition plan to meet your transition goals and assess the business situation.

The six components help you review key business elements. The Playbook helps you capture your learning and pertinent activities and events in one place, so that when opportunities arise you can make adjustments. With the information in one place, it is easier to look at scenarios and see the business interdependencies to make fact-based conclusions. You will also be able to incorporate pauses, to give you time to think and reflect on your observations. The time to think aids in assimilating the information and making any adjustment in your transition activities.

Using the six components helps maximize learning and engagement and allows you to stay organized and on track. Let's take a closer look at the six components:

1. Learn

Do not miss the opportunity to learn and get a fresh look at the business before making changes. Engage the team in taking an objective look at the business with you. Assess the business elements and avoid making hasty assumptions based on preconceived notions.

2. Lead

It can be a mistake for you to assume you can lead in this business situation in the same way you did in your last one. Transitions are a great time to make enhancements and shed old behaviors that can hold you back in the new role. Embrace new behaviors that will allow you to become more effective and efficient in carrying out the role.

3. Connect

Foster stronger relationships by getting to know the people inside the company, as well as external constituents. Understand how work gets accomplished through the interactions of all those people. Find ways to quickly build mutual trust and respect through open, candid communication. Be willing to help solve problems and commit to follow-through.

4. Assimilate

High-performing teams are critical to an organization's success. The entry of a new leader changes the dynamics of a team. It's up to you to engage with the executive team early in the process. An Assimilation Work Session (see Figures 16-1 and 16-2) is a wonderful way to facilitate dialogue and accelerate your onboarding. The session provides an opportunity to understand how the executive team currently operates. Moreover, it allows you to assess the overall talents and capabilities of the collective team. You can quickly determine if the right people are in the right roles doing the right things.

5. Communicate

Most people will want to know how the new leader will impact their work. They will be listening for signs of change. People want to quickly get to know and understand how the new leader will approach the business. Direct communication gives people the information they need and gives you the ability to see how your messages are socialized throughout the company. You can also use communication to reduce rumors and keep people focused on achieving the business's desired results.

6. Balance

A new role typically means extra hours and additional stress. Daily practices, along with attention to family and personal time, can often take a back seat to the long hours it takes to get up-to-speed in the new role. Incorporating healthy practices into your transition plan aids in the elimination of stresses and imbalances that frequently accompany a transition. Paying attention to family and personal time can give you the necessary break to stay grounded, energized, and focused.

The six key components are interrelated — they form a circle, always a strong shape — and work best using an iterative approach. Chapters 4 through 22 will provide the tools for you to create your transition plan. As you work on your transition plan, you will find yourself reviewing the various components when it makes sense for you. Similarly, as you work in one component, you will find yourself gaining strengths in another.

As noted above, each transition is unique to the business situation; you create your own transition to meet your individual needs. Figure 2-3 suggests activities that you may want to carry out in relation to each component to help you build the knowledge, relationships, and skills needed to succeed in your new role.

Executive Transition Playbook Activities

Figure 2-3

Set the Goals

- Define the business situation
- Create guiding principles for the transition
- Identify transition goals and strategy
- Align goals and strategies with new manager
- Set the tone/timing/tempo for the transition
- Create an Executive Transition Sourcebook

Learn

- Remove obstacles to learning (see Chapter 9)
- Gather information about the strategy, people, processes, organization, operations, and customers
- Get to know the products and services
- Understand the culture
- Learn about the current organizational needs and dynamics

Connect

- Identify associates' needs
- Prepare for one-on-one conversations using the Stakeholder Preparation Plan (see Figure 11-1)
- Foster relationships with direct reports, peers, senior leaders, and the Board
- Craft an Influence Map (see Chapter 9)
- Create mutual expectations
- Develop relationships with key external constituents

Assimilate

- Understand how the organization works
- Complete an Assimilation Work Session (see Figures 16-1 and 16-2)
- Engage with the Executive Team
- Get to know the team, the talent, the roles
- Understand how to participate in strategic initiatives
- Identify the right talent, right people, right skills, right roles for moving forward

Lead

- Craft your personal branding messages
- Clarify your role
- Understand your strengths and vulnerabilities
- Identify new leadership behaviors using the Leadership Plan (see Figure 7-2)
- Prepare to lead change
- Create a feedback system
- Identify the communication and coaching requirements

Communicate

- Define communication principles and strategy
- Draft a Transition Communication Plan (see Chapter 13)
- Practice and use active, conscious listening skills
- Hone skills at giving and receiving feedback
- Focus on being visible

Balance

- Incorporate Daily Practices to stay healthy and balanced (see Chapter 10)
- Attend to family matters
- Calendar in key personal events
- Set a leadership example of work/life balance
- Follow up on commitments
- Address logistics regarding moving, office and business setup
- Get involved in community endeavors

Chapter 3

Implementing the Executive Transition Playbook

If you don't know where you are going, you'll end up somewhere else.

– Yogi Berra

The Executive Transition Playbook gives structure to work through all the key steps of your transition. As you start applying the steps, you will find yourself working back and forth, returning to areas, adding to the information in the forms, and generally turning the Playbook into the tool that is appropriate for you. Remember that your transition process should give you the information you need to act effectively. Expand your plan beyond your comfort zone to ensure that you are covering all the bases.

I have found, though, that many leaders work in a specific sequence and pattern. The timeline shown in Figure 3-1 sets out a common sequence, pattern, and timing for implementing the Playbook. This timeline is just a suggested guide, but if you follow it, you will get what you need from the Playbook. Some executives start with this high-level timeline, and then develop more detailed transition activities mapped across a three- to four-month calendar. Others prefer to create more of a project plan overview that includes the key areas to focus on. Chapter 9 outlines the specific business elements to review during your transition period.

While the forms visually depict what information to consider in your Playbook, the emphasis is less on filling out the form and more on thinking through your approach and taking action.

The Executive Transition Playbook Timeline
Figure 3-1

Set Goals and Develop the Transition Plan

Planning Before Day 1	Get Acquainted Days 1–30	Connect and Learn Days 1–90
☐ Complete previous assignment	☐ Update goals, expectations & milestones	☐ Incorporate Daily Healthy Practices into schedule
☐ Begin initial research	☐ Setup & Logistics	☐ Review goals & expectations
☐ Define business situation	☐ Complete Orientation	☐ Organize business & product reviews
☐ Set transition goals & guiding principles	☐ Develop Executive Transition Playbook	☐ Schedule site visits
☐ Develop high-level transition calendar	☐ Calendar events	☐ Meet top 10 customers
☐ Outline your Learning Plan	☐ Gather all materials	☐ Cultivate relationships – use Stakeholder Preparation Tool & Influence Map
☐ Pull together personal branding information	☐ Prioritize & sequence meetings/events	☐ Complete Direct Report conversations
☐ Draft your Communication Principles	☐ Discuss goals with the boss	☐ Schedule regular check-ins with your manager
☐ Prepare yourself for change	☐ Align Leadership Plan to goals, business & personal development	☐ Complete Assimilation Work Session
☐ Map out Daily Healthy Practices	☐ Schedule Daily Healthy Practices	☐ Communicate using Communication Plan
☐ Enlist key advisors & other resources	☐ Craft Communication Plan	☐ Develop new leadership skills
☐ Seek objective transition advice from experts	☐ Communicate expectations	☐ Review, reflect & adjust plans
☐ Develop preliminary Stakeholder list	☐ Prepare for conversations using Stakeholder Preparation Plan	☐ Tap into experts & mentors for advice
	☐ Outline sections for the Executive Transition Sourcebook	☐ Capture information in Executive Transition Sourcebook
	☐ Set date for Assimilation Work Session	

Figure 3-1 *continued*

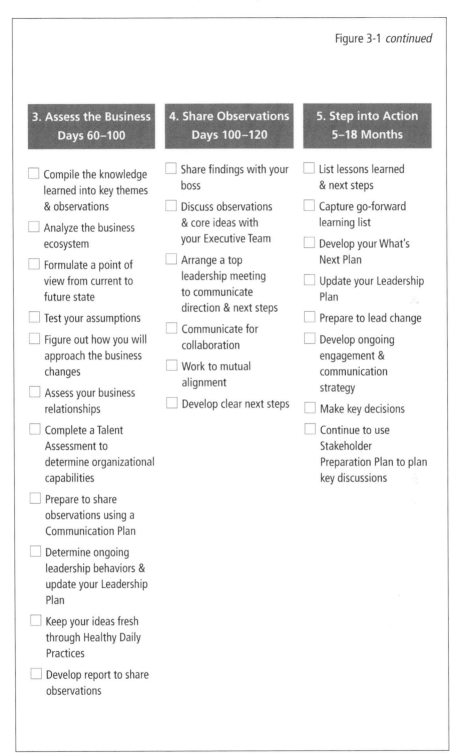

3. Assess the Business
Days 60–100

- [ ] Compile the knowledge learned into key themes & observations
- [ ] Analyze the business ecosystem
- [ ] Formulate a point of view from current to future state
- [ ] Test your assumptions
- [ ] Figure out how you will approach the business changes
- [ ] Assess your business relationships
- [ ] Complete a Talent Assessment to determine organizational capabilities
- [ ] Prepare to share observations using a Communication Plan
- [ ] Determine ongoing leadership behaviors & update your Leadership Plan
- [ ] Keep your ideas fresh through Healthy Daily Practices
- [ ] Develop report to share observations

4. Share Observations
Days 100–120

- [ ] Share findings with your boss
- [ ] Discuss observations & core ideas with your Executive Team
- [ ] Arrange a top leadership meeting to communicate direction & next steps
- [ ] Communicate for collaboration
- [ ] Work to mutual alignment
- [ ] Develop clear next steps

5. Step into Action
5–18 Months

- [ ] List lessons learned & next steps
- [ ] Capture go-forward learning list
- [ ] Develop your What's Next Plan
- [ ] Update your Leadership Plan
- [ ] Prepare to lead change
- [ ] Develop ongoing engagement & communication strategy
- [ ] Make key decisions
- [ ] Continue to use Stakeholder Preparation Plan to plan key discussions

As you read through this book, you will find information, thought-provoking questions, and worksheets to help you create your transition plan. Use the Executive Transition Playbook Activities in Figure 2-3 and the Executive Transition Playbook Timeline in Figure 3-1 as guides in developing a plan that fits your leadership style and the business.

Chapter 4

Ensuring that Your Transition Stays on Track

Leadership is the challenge to be something more
than average.

— Jim Rohn

A well-planned transition enables you to get up-to-speed and to build working relationships with your new colleagues. The conversations that take place in the transition will move beyond interview-depth discussions to the realities of running the business. Onboarding checklists are terrific management tools, but are not sufficient for executives to lead themselves and the business through the transition. The key is to build the foundation of work and contributions for years to come.

The Executive Transition Playbook is a strategic plan that incorporates both the physical components of a business transition and the personal/interpersonal aspects that help the executive cultivate new business relationships. I have found that a lack of awareness of interpersonal skills gets in the way more than technical skill gaps do. When you become more aware of your interpersonal skills and adept at improving them, you can become a more effective leader.

While a successful transition does not guarantee that you will thrive, it does create a solid foundation from which to lead. On the other hand, if you are trying to transition into a new role without a defined plan, people may believe this is how you will approach the business.

Ten Indicators that Your Transition Is Off Track

It's easy for well-intentioned leaders to get off track in their first few months, only to find they are disenfranchised and the organization has become disappointed with them. The leader then becomes isolated and struggles to be effective. What's worse is that the leader's job could be in jeopardy, and the company would have to find another way to get the work done.

How do you know if your transition is off track? Figure 4-1 discusses ten indicators to watch out for. If you recognize yourself in any of these indicators, you know that it's time to stop, identify what is going wrong, and take steps to turn your transition in the right direction.

One of the goals of this book is to help you navigate around the rapids and waterfalls and give you a process to take control of your transition into your new role. Use your time wisely to pull together the information you need to learn about the organization, establish working relationships with your stakeholders, and begin to move the business forward. In a short time, you will become established in your role and will be working successfully on meeting organizational goals.

Ten Indicators that Your Transition Is Off Track Figure 4-1

1. **Stepping out of learning mode too soon**
   Transitions are a unique opportunity to learn, inquire, and determine how to contribute. Absorb and take in all the information to make more informed decisions. Reflect on what you've learned. Before moving too quickly, look at all the options and scenarios.

2. **Becoming isolated and failing to build trusting and solid relationships**
   Make getting to know people your top priority. While you might be meeting many people, could you be isolated from the true conversations? Develop open lines of communication. Meet all your stakeholders. Listen and learn.

Figure 4-1 *continued*

3. **Making changes without sufficient understanding about how work gets done**
   Understand the organization's current culture and work patterns before you start to make changes.

4. **Thinking you can move in a different direction from your boss**
   Forge a strong relationship with your boss, and align your thinking and actions.

5. **Disregarding the social and political aspects of the organization's culture**
   Every business has its own culture and ways of working. Understand and be aware of the dynamics of social interactions and office politics in the organization, so that you can better move through these situations for the good of the organization.

6. **Saying one thing and doing another**
   Ensure that your messages are consistent, and follow through on commitments. Find ways to be authentic. Articulate and demonstrate how you lead. Pay special attention to aligning your personal brand, values, and leadership approaches with the business situation.

7. **Depending too much on what worked in the past**
   Do not assume that what you did in the past will work in your new position. As needed, expand your skills and learning to succeed in this new business situation.

8. **Failing to build new leadership skills**
   Match your leadership skills and practices to how you need to lead in your new role. Surround yourself with others who have skills and talents that complement yours.

9. **Talking too much about your previous company**
   People will wonder why you left your previous company if you continue to talk about how great it was.

10. **Acting without a clear plan**
    Develop an Executive Transition Playbook to set a strategy and structure for capturing and sequencing critical actions.

PART II

Leading Your Transition

Chapter 5

Asking for Help

We're all working together; that's the secret.

– Sam Walton

You've accepted a new role. Precious time, resources, and money have been spent to find you. You were likely hired because of your prior experience and track record. The organization is counting on you to create a thriving business. To do that, you will need the organization's support, starting with your transition.

Typically, the Human Resources department can help you with logistics, but they may not fully understand your role or be in a position to help you with all your transition needs.

If you are fortunate to get transition support, take it gladly. Otherwise, you may have to tell people clearly what you need. It is essential to start looking for the people who can help you as soon as you are onboard.

Here are three key areas where you'll want to ask for support.

1. Working with you on the Executive Transition Playbook components

Seek out others who can help you with your transition plan. Ask others where to find pertinent information to aid your learning process. Solicit advice on the areas the organization considers important to cover. Ask people to make introductions and arrange meetings to get conversations started. Seek input on how best to navigate the ins and outs of the company so that you can maximize the time you spend learning and connecting.

2. Asking for what you need

Request assistance early and often, and be clear about your needs. People in the organization may simply not know that they should be providing information, input, or support. Be aware that not everyone will be in a position to help — or want to — so be flexible about how your transition needs can be met.

3. Preparing the organization for change

Your entry signals change in the organization. If you sense that people do not understand why you have been brought on board, ask your boss or the Board to work with you to communicate the reasons for the changes. Pay attention to how people react to your entry into the role. Are people grieving over your predecessor, or are people anxious for you to get started? This input provides data about how people handle change. Use this opportunity to learn about the organization's history with change in both large and small initiatives. How did people handle the changes? Pay particular attention to the organization's culture and how work gets completed. Any changes you make will affect the ways of working and the culture of how people approach the business. Look for clues so you can anticipate any resistance and skepticism you might face when making changes in the future.

If You Need Help, but Are Afraid to Ask

Here's a secret: People tend to avoid discussing how to make a new leader's transition effective until it is too late. While a new leader is likely chosen for the role because of past performance and knowledge, there is no guarantee that the new leader will be successful in a new assignment.

Because people were obviously speaking highly of you during the recruiting process, you are entering the organization and your new role as a "superhuman" who is thought to be equipped to handle any leadership challenge. The Board or senior management will try to be polite and respectful, giving you room to figure things out for yourself. Or, by contrast, they may become so involved that you feel as if you are being micromanaged.

While the Board and others try to be helpful, they may not be capable of advising you on the nuances of the transition. You may want assistance but are afraid to ask, as this may be seen as a sign of weakness. And, unfortunately, there is the stigma that only leaders with "performance issues" seek help. You can do yourself and the organization a favor and state when you need help and what you require. When in doubt, ask for assistance. This opens the dialogue, and people around you will feel more comfortable sharing insights and giving you feedback.

Organizations can offer the necessary transition support only if they know your needs. If you require advice, find your own support, though, because this is a vulnerable time for you. If you are fortunate enough to have advisors and other confidants, seek their guidance. Additionally, ask the organization to retain the services of coaches, consultants, or others, so that you get the support you need as you work through the transition options.

Chapter 6

Gaining Clarity about Your Role

Whenever things go a bit sour in a job I'm doing,
I always tell myself, "You can do better than this."

— Dr. Seuss

Get Clear on Your Roles and Responsibilities

When you are clear on your roles and responsibilities, you can create value without questioning whether what you want to do is within your job scope. One chief marketing officer I worked with joined a company that had no written roles and responsibilities. The company simply expected leaders coming into a role to know what to do. This can create unnecessary fits and starts in terms of what a leader assumes are the role and responsibilities for the job. Clarity enables leaders to actually get the job done.

The marketing officer assumed she alone was accountable for making specific decisions for the business in her area of expertise, marketing, only to find out that her boss assumed he would be involved in the decisions. Unfortunately, her early conversations with her boss turned into uncomfortable discussions clarifying expectations, rather than useful discussions about growing the business.

Some organizations have clearly articulated roles and responsibilities; others do not. It is best to use your early time with your boss to discuss scenarios to clarify your role, including such areas as authority, decision-making, and key activities.

A RACI chart can be a useful guide to getting conversations started about who does what. RACI stands for Responsible, Accountable, Consulted, and Informed (see Figure 6-1). You and your boss can use a RACI chart to outline roles, clarify how decisions get made, define interactions between functions, and clear up ambiguities. A RACI chart is an objective way to guide conversations with your team, with peers, or with other leaders. Whether you share the RACI chart with others or use it as a personal exercise, it will help you clarify your questions and better define your role accountabilities.

RACI Chart

Figure 6-1

RACI is a great tool for assessing roles and responsibilities, especially during times of change. The RACI chart provides a clear, visual representation of the activities mapped against each role. It clarifies how work gets accomplished, thus avoiding the potential of misinterpretation. Identify the business activities and mark the columns alongside each activity as to who is R, A, C, and I.

Responsible   Person assigned to the work and working on the activity

Accountable   Person who makes the final decision and is the ultimate owner of the work

Consulted   Person who must be consulted before a decision or action is taken

Informed   Person who needs to be informed of the decision or action

BUSINESS ACTIVITIES	ROLE					
	Board	CEO	CFO	CMO	HR	President
Activity 1						
Activity 2						
Activity 3						
Activity 4						
Activity 5						

Set Goals with Your Boss

In most businesses, even the chief executive officer is accountable to someone whom I will loosely call "the boss." Your own boss has a vested interest in your achieving success. Your role is situation dependent and will require coordination of your goals and expectations with those of your boss. Try not to be surprised if the realities and the focus of your role change from when you first discussed the role in the interview process. While any strategic and visionary ideas you have may be relevant and useful, the realities of delivering the business targets take precedence and drive your priorities. So collaborate with your boss by working through a goal-setting exercise together. As you develop clarity of direction and a sense of how you will work together, you will be setting the foundation for a solid working relationship with your boss. There may be others who can give you insights on how to best work with your boss.

Figure 6-2 sets out the framework to prepare for goal alignment and business review discussions with your boss. Depending on your reporting relationships, this template can be used when talking with Board members or the CEO. A similar template may be useful for your direct reports to fill out when they are working with you. Here is an overview of the parts of the business review framework:

Business Review

Use every opportunity to stay in lockstep with your boss regarding the business. Put your business plan on one page for easy discussions with your boss and others. Use the one-pager to reconnect and make sure the business activities are aligned with the company's mission, vision, and strategy.

- Do you and your boss have the same perspectives on the business?
- Where do you agree, and where do you see things differently?

Take note of any sage advice your boss gives you about your transition, the people, and the business.

Performance Indicators

Understand how success in the business is measured and how you will ultimately be measured. Get clear about your goals, as well as your boss's

Goals and Business Review One-Pager	Figure 6-2
Business Review:	
Performance Indicators:	
Strategic Initiatives:	
Opportunities and Challenges:	
Engaging Others and Managing Relationships:	
Resource Requirements:	
Roles, Expectations, and Working Together:	
Professional Development:	
Actions and Next Steps:	

performance goals, as sometimes these can be similar or different.

- What goals and metrics does your boss have for you, for the transition, and for the business?
- Are these the same goals and metrics you expected?
- How can you align your goals and metrics with those of your boss?
- What scorecards or dashboards are used to monitor the business?

If the business doesn't use a scorecard or some type of dashboard, create one. This will help you easily review the business's metrics and performance.

Strategic Initiatives

Provide updates on key initiatives you're working on, and outline how your boss can support these efforts. All too often, there will be far too many initiatives, so it's better to prioritize and focus on what will give the most positive impact to the business. Check with your boss on what's important and what can be postponed.

Opportunities and Challenges

Use the time you spend with your boss to identify challenges and find workable solutions. Your boss is one of the few people who can relate to the challenges both you and the business face. Surface any items regarding the business, leadership, or your role. Develop a way to resolve issues and concerns with your boss — sooner rather than later. Listen to your boss's advice and counsel on ways to take advantage of the various challenges and opportunities.

Engaging Others and Managing Relationships

Seek your boss's guidance and assistance in identifying key relationships both inside and outside the company, and in making introductions to cultivate strong relationships. What insights does your boss have about forging these relationships? Can your boss assist with framing important conversations? Are there specific people in the company who are considered the "informal leaders" or "key influencers" that you should get to know? Who can help you in tapping into the organizational knowledge and in engaging others? Discuss strategies to engage the organization in upcoming changes.

Resource Requirements

What resources do you need to help make the business more successful? Such resources may include requests for additional staffing, financial support, freedom to act, clarification of policies and procedures, information technology, or any other essentials of the business.

Roles, Expectations, and Working Together

One of your roles is actually to enable others — including your boss — to be successful. Get clear on your roles and responsibilities, so that you are aligned around how you will work together. How does your boss prefer to communicate and be kept informed? Arrange for regular check-ins to keep each other informed. Determine how you and your boss best complement one another. Are there certain things that annoy your boss? When and how does your boss want to be actively involved? What's the best way to work on joint initiatives to avoid any confusion or overduplication of efforts? Solicit feedback so you can make adjustments as appropriate.

Professional Development

Gain your boss's feedback and insights on how you are transitioning into the new role. Which behaviors do you need to change, or to adopt? Which skills do you need to acquire to perform well in the new role? Build personal development actions into your transition plan.

Not every boss will be available for regular meetings. If you have a clear idea of what you want to cover, you will be able to better utilize your discussions in the allotted time.

Chapter 7

Preparing to Lead in Your New Role

Pay attention, as your thoughts become words.
Your words become actions. Your actions become habits.
Your habits become your character. Your character
becomes your destiny.

– Chinese proverb

Match Your Leadership Approach to the Business

What you say and do affects the actions of others. Even what you *don't* say speaks volumes. People count on clear directions and guidance to enable them to do their work. Leaders who inspire and motivate others will surely see their businesses thrive. It's not a matter of their charisma; it's about understanding how to set clear direction, provide meaningful work, and help others to perform at their very best.

You cannot assume that your leadership approach and actions will work in any role and in any organization. As your role changes, so should your leadership approach. Begin to cultivate self-awareness around how your thoughts and actions play a role in how you lead others. When you are aware of the impact your actions have on others, you can self-regulate what you say and do to bring out the best in those around you.

Transitioning into a new role is a perfect time to assess how you are leading others. You will always find an area to develop or improve. Consider revisiting past performance reviews, leadership assessments, and feedback, and also seek input from others who know you well in a working role.

Personal SWOT Analysis

You may be familiar with a SWOT analysis in assessing your business. I recommend that you conduct a personal SWOT analysis — identifying and assessing your Strengths, Weaknesses, Opportunities, and Threats — to understand your current approach to leading as you take on a new role. As an executive, you most likely have a preferred working style. Doing a SWOT analysis can shed light on your leadership strengths and personal preferences, and can pinpoint areas in which you might become even more effective. As your role expands and the business environment changes, your actions must change, too.

Your personal SWOT analysis can guide your approach to leading in the new organization. You can identify areas to focus on to take advantage of your talents and the current opportunities. You can also see where you will need to rely on others for their skills and talents. Use your transition to make needed changes in your approach.

Figure 7-1 outlines questions to review as you conduct your analysis. As you answer the questions, identify your leadership behaviors that will be beneficial in your new role — and those you should stop using.

As you move to a more-senior role, you may have to shift your behaviors subtly, but significantly. What worked in your former role may no longer be appropriate. Others in the company can help you identify when to make these shifts.

Open lines of communication with people you trust, to get candid feedback on what you're doing well and where you are keeping others from doing their best work. Performance reviews, leadership assessments, and feedback are great sources of information. Family and friends can also offer valuable insights into your personal leadership abilities, which likely relate to how you will lead the business.

Personal SWOT Analysis Questions

Figure 7-1

Strengths	Weaknesses
◆ Which skills and characteristics do you consider to be your strengths? ◆ What do you do better than anyone else? ◆ What do other people see as your strengths?	◆ What are your vulnerabilities? ◆ What tasks do you usually avoid? ◆ What do others see as your weaknesses? ◆ What negative work habits or traits do you have that could hold you back?

Opportunities	Threats
◆ What trends do you see? How can you take advantage of them? ◆ Do you see any upcoming changes that you can take advantage of? ◆ What are you hearing from your network?	◆ What obstacles do you currently face in this role? ◆ Do either the changing work environment or various technology advancements intimidate you? ◆ Could any of your strengths or weaknesses lead to threats?

Identify Leadership Behaviors for Performing at Your Best

The results from the personal SWOT analysis, along with other feedback, can give you a perspective on your current leadership behaviors. This information can also provide insights into certain behaviors you need to either develop or improve. Use the worksheet in Figure 7-2 to organize this input and start planning your leadership behavior in your new role.

Leadership Plan Worksheet

Figure 7-2

What is expected of me in this role?

Personal SWOT Analysis

Strengths	Weaknesses

Opportunities	Threats

Leadership behaviors to:

Continue doing	Start doing	Stop doing

My leadership actions to lead in the new organization:

The behaviors I am likely to overrely on, at the expense of learning new behaviors:

At this point, you are capturing ideas on how to approach your new role. Keep your analysis simple: Focus on the one or two things that seem to be the top priorities. As you complete this exercise, make sure you relate the behaviors to your role and responsibilities as well as to the expectations of your company and boss. When you are in meetings and interacting with others, become more aware of how your comments and actions affect others. Could you deliver the same messages using different language, tone, and tenor and still get your points across? Often it's not the message that bothers others but how that message was communicated and how people are supported over time.

This new approach may not feel comfortable at first. New behaviors require practice if they are to become habit. Identify which actions are needed to reinforce and cultivate new behaviors so that they can become part of your leadership toolkit.

Chapter 8

Communicating Your Personal Brand

*The greatest advantage of speaking the truth is that you
don't have to remember what you said.*

– Anonymous

A good way to connect with others is through communicating your
personal brand — who you are, what you stand for, and what you
bring to your new role. Colleagues will be interested in both your
business accomplishments and your personal interests, including
your business background, family activities, leadership style, values,
and what they can expect from you.

Elements of Your Personal Brand

Collect the information you want to share, and develop messages to
communicate on the following points.

Your Business Background

Be ready to share your business background through succinct, clear
stories that provide the context for who you are and why you will
be effective in this new role.

Charting your career history line can provide a helpful visual image.
Depending on the audience, you can pick out highlights that would
help others understand who you are and how you lead. Keep it short
and simple. This isn't the time to monopolize the conversation. Give
people a high-level overview to establish your credibility and share
your expertise. Your stories should include what you did, why you did

it, how you did it, and what was accomplished. You can use your stories as a springboard to ask others questions about their experiences.

Personal and Family Interests and Activities

People want to find common ground on which they can relate to you. When people feel they know you, they will get a sense of what to expect from you and how you will react in business situations that involve them. Pull together a set of key points you want to share with people about your personal and family interests.

Leadership Values

One of the best ways to present your leadership approach is to share your values. Values express how you like to work with and interact with others. Values offer insights into what is important to you and what others can expect in their interactions with you. When people know what you value, they can tailor their actions to follow your lead. If your actions and values are not aligned, people lose confidence and trust in you. Identify three to five core values that shape the way you lead and work. Develop statements and tell stories about these values that help others understand what you mean.

Your Personal Brand and Your Value Proposition

People want to know what special value you bring to the business and how best to work with you. A personal brand describes how you differentiate yourself and how you contribute to the organization. At this stage of your career, you probably can articulate your brand in many ways. A new role is a great time to refresh how you talk about yourself.

You can articulate your personal brand by developing your own value proposition statement. Make sure you write one, as this can also become your elevator introduction (what you say to others about yourself during a 30-second ride). As you develop your value proposition, you can ask yourself:

- Who am I as a leader?
- What is my purpose?
- Why do I do what I do?
- What are my core leadership skills?
- How does my leadership affect others?

Your answers will give you the input to write two to four inspiring sentences that form your personal brand and value proposition.

Develop Core Messages or Guiding Principles

Your fellow workers expect a new leader to bring a fresh perspective and point of view to the role and the organization. You can help them learn about you and your approach by developing core messages and sharing them with others. These may be the statements, or mantras, you say when talking about how you want to operate the business. Some leaders call them business principles.

Examples of core messages include:

- Understand the business from outside in
- Build on recent success and brand strength
- Create a culture that cultivates a winning team
- We will go slow, to go fast
- Work with a sense of urgency, passion, and commitment
- While I cannot promise you anything, I will always bring you my best effort

Clearly, the core messages you want to share depend on the business situation, your leadership preferences, and how you wish to operate the business. Your core messages may change when you move from your initial transition period to leading in the future.

Establish Expectations

Set mutual expectations, so that people know where they stand. You probably have some favorite expectations that have helped prior groups work with you. What you expect in your first months in your role may change after you learn more about the business situation. But be clear about your expectations, and identify what you want

---

Example of New Leader Expectations   Figure 8-1

What you can expect from me:	What I expect from you:
◆ Listen and learn	◆ Find ways for us to work as one company
◆ Support you and your team	◆ Share information and make your thinking visible
◆ Foster a collaborative, safe environment that encourages diverse ideas	◆ Create a motivating environment for your people
◆ Provide clear direction	◆ Support decisions that we make as a team
◆ Help you think through business issues	◆ Come prepared to talk about business issues and opportunities
◆ Remove the barriers and obstacles to accomplishing work	◆ Provide solutions, not just problems
◆ Provide candid feedback and be open to your feedback	◆ Challenge the status quo
◆ Communicate and share information	◆ Use facts to make decisions
◆ Facilitate discussions and decision-making	◆ Provide ongoing feedback to me and others
◆ Allow you to run your business	◆ Communicate, and no surprises
◆ Ask questions, a lot of them	
◆ Promote healthy discussions	

---

others to do to support you both in the transition and afterward — while always leaving space to revisit your expectations.

Figure 8-1 presents examples of expectations of a leader in transition, while Figure 8-2 suggests a template for organizing these expectations as well as the other personal branding information you want to communicate.

Communicating Your Personal Brand	Figure 8-2
My Business Background	
Personal/Family Interests and Activities	
My Leadership Values	
Personal Brand (Value Proposition)	
Core Messages or Guiding Principles	
Stories to Link Experiences, Values, and Leadership	
What You Can Expect of Me	
What I Ask of You	

Chapter 9

Learning about the Business

Leadership and learning are indispensable to each other.

— John F. Kennedy

Leaders starting in a new role can be so anxious to get going that they miss opportunities to gather information about the business. You will want to use your transition time to gather information, ask questions, dig deep, and study the business.

Remove Obstacles to Learning

Before you set out to learn about the business, you will need to clear your mind of obstacles that can interfere with your objective learning. During times of change, it's easy to want to quickly sort through information so you can make comparisons and judgments to build your understanding. Work to look at the business with fresh eyes and notice if you find yourself making any of the following obstacles to learning:

1. Discounting Ideas and Concepts

When ideas and concepts do not fit your current way of thinking, you may find yourself dismissing them. While you are learning about the business, keep your biases in check and look for the objective truth about the business. Focus on understanding what people are telling you, take good notes, and consider what is being said. Listen to different perspectives with an open mind.

2. Low Levels of Presence

Your coworkers know when you are not truly listening. They expect you to be on your best behavior during the transition and to show a level of interest. The last thing they want is to see you get flustered, act inappropriately in a situation, or fail to pay attention. Remain present, as you talk with people and gather information.

3. Arrogance and Superiority

If you come into your new role expecting that you know all the answers, you can seem to be intellectually closed to the ideas and information people are presenting to you. If people perceive that you have a set agenda, they will stop sharing information with you; they may even resist the changes you are bringing to the organization. It's best to check your ego at the door and find common ground with those throughout the company.

4. Fear of Failure

As you are stepping into your new role, you may feel anxiety about entering unfamiliar territory. Some of your fears may drive stronger performance, but many fears will paralyze you and keep you from learning and entering fully into your new role. Executives rarely express their fears. Acknowledging, at least to yourself, that your fears exist and then doing something to address them helps to smooth your transition from the unknown to the known. When you face your fears, you can open up learning opportunities for yourself.

5. Ineffective Learning Styles

When you understand how you learn and absorb information, you can make better use of your time in gathering the input you need. If you are clear on how you best learn, you can accelerate your learning by incorporating appropriate activities into your transition plan.

Gather Information about the Business

Use your transition period to take a deep dive and gain a 360-degree view of the business. As you look at the business, see how things fit together at an enterprise level, as well as at the divisional, regional, country, and functional levels. Identify what needs to be similar across the organization and what requires local strategies.

Gather as much information as you can, and be sure to look at the business from various perspectives. This will allow you to observe how things are actually working.

By pulling the information together and taking an enterprise view, you may find other solutions that weren't evident when looking at the business by individual functions and segments. Look at the business from different vantage points — top to bottom, bottom to top, and cross-organizationally. Notice how well, or how poorly, the business is executing the strategy. Reviewing the business from several perspectives will uncover areas that need attention. Keep a balance between high-level views and a deep dive into the specifics. Notice when you find yourself focusing too much in one area or getting into too much detail, or even just skimming the surface of an important issue.

You can employ many models and ways of looking at the various business elements. Figure 9-1 shows a simple model that depicts the key business areas that comprise a business system. Use this model to create a learning plan for gathering information about each aspect of the business.

The questions in Figures 9-2 are meant to start you thinking about the key areas in your new business ecosystem. Carefully reviewing this table is a crucial step: You may believe that you already know

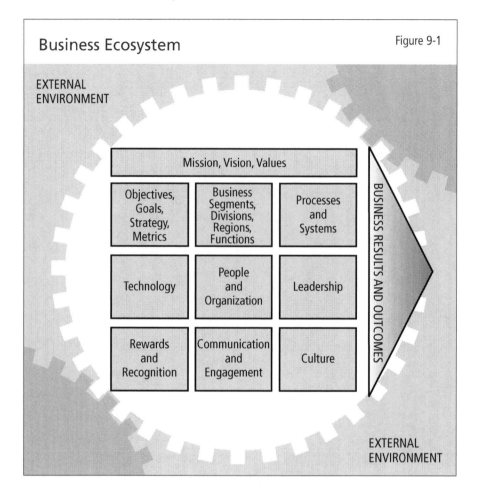

Business Ecosystem
Figure 9-1

EXTERNAL ENVIRONMENT

Mission, Vision, Values

Objectives, Goals, Strategy, Metrics

Business Segments, Divisions, Regions, Functions

Processes and Systems

Technology

People and Organization

Leadership

Rewards and Recognition

Communication and Engagement

Culture

BUSINESS RESULTS AND OUTCOMES

EXTERNAL ENVIRONMENT

some of these business considerations, or at least know how to gather data about each one. Nevertheless, do take a consultative approach to systematically review each area. You will likely see more by using an objective view. Be sure to investigate the interactions and interdependencies between all the business elements. Chances are that, if you are new to the company or division, you will want to cover each area in depth. If you are expanding your role, it's helpful to look at each of these areas with fresh eyes.

Business Ecosystem Considerations

Figure 9-2

Mission, Vision, Values

- Review the company's mission, vision, and values.
- What is the history behind the organization's vision, mission, and values?
- Have these been adopted throughout the organization?
- How are the mission, vision, and values visible in everyday work?
- How do colleagues express their values?

Objectives, Goals, Strategy, Metrics

- What is the organization's operating model?
- What are its objectives, strategy, metrics, and operating plans?
- How does the organization use metrics to run the business?
- What annual strategic planning process does it use?

Business Segments, Divisions, Regions, Functions

- How do the strategies and activities of each function, region, and department support the corporate strategy?
- How does work get done cross-functionally?
- What are the centers of excellence?
- What areas are lagging?
- How do the functions work together?
- How do divisions or business units work together?
- How much discussion occurs cross-functionally?

Processes and Systems

- What are the organization's core business processes?
- Are these processes documented?
- Are they followed?
- Are there points at which the processes fall apart or get changed by employees?
- What are the decision-making protocols?
- What are the standard operating procedures?

Figure 9-2 *continued*

Technology

- How does the organization use technology today?
- What technology platforms are being used?
- How does the technology strategy align with the corporate strategy?
- What knowledge management system is used to share information across the organization?

People and Organization

- How is the organization structured?
- Are competencies, roles, and responsibilities clearly defined?
- What is the company's talent management strategy?
- Is there a formalized succession planning process?
- What compensation and reward programs are in place?
- What learning and development programs are available for employees?
- How engaged and motivated are the organization's people?
- How is employee engagement measured?

Leadership

- How does the organization approach leadership development?
- Who are the current leaders and rising stars?
- Who are the high-potential employees?
- What leadership development programs are available?
- How well does the management team work together?
- What is the talent succession planning process?
- How is this plan managed?
- Are there any leadership issues that will inhibit the business progress?

Rewards and Recognition

- How does the organization handle rewards and recognition?
- How does the organization provide feedback, and are the feedback systems aligned with the strategy and goals?
- How are the rewards and recognitions systems working?
- What behaviors do these systems drive?

Figure 9-2 *continued*

Communication and Engagement

- ◆ How does the organization communicate?
- ◆ What communication tools are used?
- ◆ Are the communications effective?
- ◆ Are the messages consistent?
- ◆ What do people say about the communication and leadership interactions? Too little? Too much? Too formal or informal?
- ◆ What communications support will you have?
- ◆ How do people expect you to communicate?

Culture

- ◆ How would you describe the organization's culture?
- ◆ How does work get done?
- ◆ What subcultures have you identified, and how would you describe each?
- ◆ How are decisions made?
- ◆ What are the authority protocols?
- ◆ What actions are reinforced or discouraged by leaders, processes, people, and systems?
- ◆ Where is the culture of the organization most prevalent?

Business Results and Outcomes

- ◆ How are results reported?
- ◆ Does the company use specific scorecards, metrics, or data to manage the business?

External Environment

- ◆ Who are the key external stakeholders?
- ◆ What impacts do they have on the organization?
- ◆ Who is important for you to meet in your first three months?
- ◆ How do the external constituents (customers, consumers, shareholders, suppliers, vendors, community, government, regulators, and competitors) affect the organization?
- ◆ What are the expectations of Board members, customers, markets, and others?
- ◆ What issues should you know about before you start connecting with people?
- ◆ Who can assist you with introductions?

Make a list of the areas you wish to learn more about and the individuals and groups who can help you with this learning. Figure 9-3 is a worksheet on which you can capture the particular business items you wish to learn about. Be as specific as possible. Create questions to prepare for discussions with others. Notice if there are business elements you seem to gloss over. These could be areas that you need to learn more about or pay more attention to.

Executive Transition Playbook Activity List

Figure 9-3

Business Element	My Learning Actions	Who Can Help Me?
Mission, Vision, Values		
Objectives, Goals, Strategy, Metrics		
Business Segments, Divisions, Regions, Functions		
Processes and Systems		
Technology		
People and Organization		
Leadership		
Rewards and Recognition		
Communication and Engagement		
Culture		
Business Results and Outcomes		
External Environment		

One company president I worked with avoided looking at the business's processes and focused instead on a new business strategy. After some coaxing, he reviewed several key processes. It became apparent the processes weren't aligned with the strategy. He saw that adjusting the strategy alone wasn't going to solve the problems. So he and his team created a new strategy and modified the processes to fit the strategy. The alignment of the two business elements enabled his people to work on the right things to achieve the business targets.

Use a three-month timeline to outline a high-level schedule, then match your business learning activities with your meeting schedule. The key is to give yourself enough time to analyze the business and meet key people. Depending on your situation, the time needed to develop a working knowledge of the business will vary. Prepare questions and ask for information to review ahead of time, so that you can use key meetings and touch points to delve into each area. Sort, sequence, and align the learning checklist with the meetings and interactions, then fill in the gaps through additional conversations.

Learning is an iterative process. Different information will present itself as you engage in a series of meetings and interactions. Pay special attention to areas that may not get readily populated with information, as these are potential blind spots.

Using these questions and worksheets in Figures 9-2 and 9-3 helps you collect all your questions and use different venues and forums to discuss a variety of topics. Be sure to look at the timing and sequencing of your meetings to maximize your learning.

Some leaders like to create an Executive Transition Sourcebook, which is a binder with sections and tabs to collect all the pertinent information. Others use an electronic version. The Executive Transition Sourcebook is described in detail in Chapter 21.

Understand the Culture, Agendas, and Politics

"Ways of working" and other cultural nuances are typically learned by trial and error. During the transition period, become a student of the organization's culture and make deliberate efforts to assess the impact of that culture on business results.

- What are the company's values? Are they visible in everyday work discussions?
- How do people express those values?
- What is never tolerated?
- Who in the organization best exhibits the values?
- What will you need to do to adapt to the culture?

Through direct observation and discussions, gain an understanding of how the organization operates. This information will help you enormously when it's time to implement change.

New leaders frequently shy away from or ignore office politics, hoping they will disappear or not be a problem. Instead, you need to identify the people (every organization has them!) who act politically and carry personal agendas. Find out what initiatives and agendas they are promoting, and why. Listen for the topics that easily offend people. How are historical events inhibiting people's ability to work together? When you become aware of the dynamics of the social interactions and personal agendas that exist, you will be more able to manage these situations for the greater good of the business.

I advise my clients to talk less and observe more in the early days in a new role. The little things you notice will add up, till you can define the existing culture. Ask yourself a series of hard questions in your first few weeks and months: Do meetings start and end on time? How are difficult discussions handled? How are things done, and how are people engaged with each other? How is information shared, authority deployed, and decisions made? How are the company's values socialized throughout the organization, and what are other characteristics of the business's culture?

Use your transition period to learn how others work, before you try to impose your own methodologies and techniques on the organization. Once you demonstrate that you understand the current culture, then you have earned the right to help shift and shape the organization into a better future.

Create an Influence Map

Work is rarely done alone. Most of the time, leaders are interacting, exchanging information, and providing work products to one another. Leaders may be comfortable deciding on their own actions. However, are such individuals actually aware of how their actions influence what others do and say? Remember that key influencers may not necessarily be in senior positions.

As part of your learning, endeavor to understand how work in the organization is influenced by others. This influence can come from a variety of places — hierarchies, friendships, old connections, past patterns, and so forth. Sometimes these key influencers can be helpful, and at other times they can stagnate and block work progress. Indeed, these unofficial influences can mean the difference between success and failure for you and the business.

When you understand how influence works in the organization, you can navigate through it more efficiently. You can see whom you should work with and which relationships will be important to develop. You can even use the influencers to communicate your own messages and expectations.

As you gather information about the organization, you should be able to see both the official and the unofficial patterns of influence. To help you get started with this learning, follow these steps:

- Identify the people who influence the business. These may be people directly or indirectly engaged in the business. They are not necessarily the decision-makers.
- Describe the role of each.
- Determine whom these people influence. What connections do they have, and why?
- Assess the strength of the influence on a scale of high, medium, or low.
- Learn about the history of the relationships and patterns among them.
- Anticipate what the influencers will expect from you.
- Create a plan to address any areas of concern.

Often, you can enhance the working relationships, to benefit the business. First, though, start by understanding how information, ideas, and work products are currently shared among all parties.

Chapter 10

Creating Balance through Healthy Daily Practices

I cannot make my days longer, so I strive to make them better.

– Henry David Thoreau

Times of transition can be hectic and stressful as leaders move out of their comfort zone. This is why "Balance" is one of the blocks in the Executive Transition Playbook. When you incorporate your personal activities and obligations into your transition, you can get a full picture of your schedule and commitments, and you will be creating the circumstances under which the business, you, and your family can flourish.

Healthy Practices for Peak Performance

The pressures of a new job and transition can test work/life balance. Energy, focus, and clarity are essential as you face a high learning curve and expectations of high performance. A transition, therefore, is an excellent time to reaffirm or reset your health habits.

Many leaders already have a set of healthy daily practices; if you do, you need to continue your practices during this time of change. Unfortunately, while most leaders have good intentions, their time commitments do not always let them follow a healthy regime.

I have found that exceptional leaders aren't "super people." Rather, they have found that daily healthy practices keep them at the top of their game. They have built their life and work around the healthy daily practices that help them stay energized, fresh, and balanced, so that they can tackle what they need to face in business and in life.

The marketplace is filled with programs to help individuals bring a healthy balance to the physical, emotional, mental, and spiritual body. There are companies incorporating health and wellness programs into employees' work lives as a way to reduce stress, improve health, and enhance productivity. These programs are designed to teach individuals how to manage their energy levels through healthy practices in order to maximize performance levels. The key is to use the tools regularly.

If you are not already following a set of healthy daily practices, I recommend that you start incorporating them into your schedule. The key is to do things that keep you at your peak performance. Below are daily practices I find most beneficial, especially during times of change:

- Exercising at least 20 to 30 minutes a day — a brisk walk at lunch can make a huge difference
- Getting up early to plan the critical tasks and to get energized to manage the day's events
- Eating healthy foods
- Staying hydrated
- Sleeping at least seven to nine hours per night to allow your body and mind to rest and regenerate
- Regaining balance through deep breathing
- Showing gratitude and providing others positive feedback every day
- Finding a few minutes of silence and quiet time, whether through meditation or other techniques
- Capturing your thoughts in a journal
- Taking breaks from your electronic devices

Set an Example

As the new leader, you are setting the tone, pace, and cadence you want in the business. It's one thing to discuss work/life balance; it's another to live it. If you work long hours and weekends, people around you will start to follow suit. Your actions will turn into unintended expectations for others to meet. Long hours do not always equate to better results, however; these long hours may exhaust the creative minds around you. For some period of time, it will take longer hours for you to get up-to-speed. However, take care not to make these long hours a habit, as they can lead to a downward spiral of productivity. It's important to work smartly and efficiently. And remember that sometimes a break can help spark new ideas.

If you want a healthy, creative, and focused organization, you need to set an example to create this environment. Your actions, your values, and the way you work can all show others how you want them to work.

People will be watching you for signs of how you work and what you value. Some may even start to copy you. In Chapter 7, I explained how to create a leadership plan that may include behaviors you want to instill throughout the business. I recommend being aware of your actions and determining whether they exhibit the example you want to set.

Attend to Family

Family and friends can help keep you grounded. They have different expectations than do your business colleagues. They can help you through the transition, if you let them know how they can help.

Savvy leaders build support systems. They make sure the important activities in their personal lives are incorporated into their Executive Transition Playbook. You should do the same. When all your activities are captured and sequenced into a timeline, it becomes easier to manage both your personal and your professional needs. Set aside time to keep up with personal activities and important events, and to spend quality time with your family during (and after) the transition.

Here are some ways you can engage your family in your transition:

- Set mutual expectations with family members.
- Listen to how your family is coping with the change. Recognize that your new role may or may not be as welcome to others as it is to you.
- Identify the personal activities that will need attention. Carve out quality time to interact with family and friends.
- Keep your family informed about time commitments and travel schedules.
- Identify others who may be able to help at home with ongoing activities.
- Incorporate your personal activities into your transition plan, so that you can manage the entire transition period in one place. When there are shifts in your business schedule, you can see how they may affect your personal schedule.
- Do not simply forego community activities and commitments. Rather, transition your responsibilities to others.
- If you need to move to a new location, involve your family in planning and organizing the move. This will help them recognize and organize the changes the move will bring to their own plans and activities.

PART III

Working with Others in the Transition

Chapter 11

Making First Impressions Count

The more you extend kindness to yourself, the more it will become your automatic response from others.

— Wayne Dyer

It's true, people will be quick to assess you by the first impressions you make. People will look for answers to their questions about you in your opening introductions. Even if they know you, they will be curious about how you plan to approach the business. Entering the new role is an opportunity to make new relationships or build on existing ones. This starts with the first impressions you make in this new role.

Relationships can take time to develop and cultivate. In a transition, it can feel a bit like speed dating; however, these "dates" are with people you hope to be working with for a long time. So make your first impressions and subsequent interactions count. When you outline how to approach initial conversations with people, you can quickly build a level of rapport and trust in the dialogue and exchanges. Leaders often get distracted by the activities in the transition, causing the building of key relationships to stall.

Stakeholder Preparation Plan

A useful tool to prepare for conversations and interactions is a Stakeholder Preparation Plan. Figure 11-1 shows a sample plan. The Stakeholder Preparation Plan is a vehicle for thinking through messages and tone ahead of time. When you plan how you are going to interact with others, conversations will be more productive. Better discussions aid in forging stronger relationships.

An Example of a Stakeholder Preparation Plan Figure 11-1

Individual or Group: Mary (CFO)

General Information

♦ Dedicated 20 years to the company, all in finance.

♦ Works well with peers.

♦ People rely on Mary to help make business decisions.

Meeting Purpose

♦ Brief introduction with Mary to get the conversation started. Help put her at ease with the transition and determine how to work together.

Messages and Talking Points

♦ I have heard so much about your contributions.

♦ Financial discipline is important to me in running a healthy business.

♦ I will look to you to help make business decisions.

♦ I need your help to get my arms around the financial statements.

Reactions and Concerns

♦ Earnings are not keeping up with revenue growth. Spending continues to be an issue.

♦ The leadership team has been fractured, and the business segment presidents don't work well with one another.

♦ We don't invest enough in our people.

Their Questions

♦ How will you work to get the organization more focused on profits?

♦ What are your plans to grow the business?

♦ How can I help you in the transition?

Questions to Ask

♦ What is important to you?

♦ What do I need to focus on right now?

♦ How will you and I work together?

Actions

♦ Review Mary's inquiry regarding promotion opportunities.

♦ Set up meetings with the financial team.

♦ Initiate business reviews.

♦ Review the forecasting model.

♦ Look into management team dynamics.

Start by identifying the individuals or groups you want to get to know, then prepare the key messages, questions, and comments for each stakeholder group. Your list of stakeholders could include:

- The Board of Directors
- Your boss
- Peers
- Direct reports
- Key executives
- Division or department heads
- Managers of essential functions
- Employees/Associates
- Customers
- Partners
- Investor community
- Key suppliers
- Key external influencers (such as government officials and regulatory agencies)

The Stakeholder Preparation Plan outlines a framework to prepare for discussions with each stakeholder or stakeholder group. For each, use the following questions:

General Information

What is the purpose of this conversation? What do I want this individual to know and feel as a result of our discussion? What interests and excites them about the business? What do they value? How do they prefer to be engaged in the business activities?

Messages and Talking Points

What does this individual or group need to hear from me? What personalized messages do I want to convey in my conversations? What is the preferred communication style? How will we work together? What expectations do I have?

Reactions and Concerns

How will they react to the messages? What will they be most concerned about? What kinds of indicators will show they are engaged in my messages? Where might there be some resistance from this individual or group?

Questions from Them

What questions do I expect from the individual or group, and how should I respond?

Questions to Ask

What questions do I have for this individual or group? What do they need to know for us to be able to move things forward?

Actions

What actions should I or others take to help support this individual or group?

In Chapter 17, I suggest a sequence of conversations with direct reports, in which you can gather information and start building those working relationships. The Stakeholder Preparation Plan is a handy tool to prepare for these discussions.

Chapter 12

Opening the Channels of Communication

You are responsible not only for what you say, but also for what you do not say.

— Martin Luther

Communication Takes on a New Meaning

By now, you may be picking up how important it is to communicate effectively with colleagues and stakeholders throughout your transition. The role and title you have been assigned may be intimidating to some of them, even if you do not actually think you are an intimidating person. They will appreciate clear, concise, and engaging communication, which is an essential tool for any leader.

The same message you deliver may have to be repeated many times before people absorb and assimilate its meaning. You may get tired of saying the same thing and move on to a second message before people have fully absorbed and acted on the first one. Plan to stay on message, even when you grow weary of saying the same thing over and over again. By the time people start to repeat your message, thinking of it almost as a mantra, the organization should be well on its way to implementing the underlying changes.

Expect what you say to be amplified or distorted as your messages cascade throughout the organization. A single negative comment can send the organization swirling. It helps to convey positive, forward-looking messages that others can easily repeat and act on. Morale can dip during times of change, and people may lose their focus on the business. This is a time to keep the messages simple, clear, and consistent, so people stay focused on what matters. Also, use genuine praise to motivate people to keep moving in the right direction.

Check to see if the messages are getting through. You will want to test whether the direction is clear and whether people actually know what to do. From the beginning, find ways to make connections with all areas of the company, and check whether people are actually hearing the messages. Test your messages by asking questions. You can best learn about problems and issues in the company by asking people what they think and what they are experiencing. Make it a habit to regularly ask people what they need to solve the business challenges.

Eliminating the Filters

Even your most well-intended colleagues may filter the messages they hear, so as not to bother you with any questions about the details. People will quickly figure out what you want to hear and what disturbs you, and they will make the adjustments. Unless you do something to keep the lines of communication open, you could find yourself farther and farther away from the actual work.

The isolation makes it more difficult to thoroughly understand what is going on in the organization, and the flow of information becomes compromised. With the pulls on your time and the limited interactions, it grows difficult to stay in touch with the realities of the business. Your efforts to engage associates with the right levels of communication may fall short.

So make it your goal to remove the filters and keep the lines of communication open. Take care that your actions do not undermine your interest in having frank dialogue. If you find yourself seeing only one side of the issue, take the time to broaden communications to see all sides of the issue.

Everything Communicates

A leader's actions can speak volumes, especially when communication is limited. It's easy to find yourself spending most of your time with a few individuals or departments and less time engaging with the entire enterprise. A new leader such as yourself can easily become distracted with obligations, which significantly reduces the level of interactions.

People can also misinterpret your actions. Approach every connection as an opportunity to convey a message, to clarify the strategy, and to help people and the company move in the right direction. Convey messages through your actions. Consider the effect of even the most mundane actions, such as where you eat lunch (the cafeteria or at your desk), where you park your car, whether you fly commercial or use the corporate jet, or which facilities and customers you decide to visit. None of these actions are right or wrong, but recognize that others will try to read more into your actions and may even want to emulate your habits.

When a leader isn't communicating effectively, employees complain that they haven't heard from the boss. People want to receive messages, especially when those messages come directly from you. They want messages that speak to their issues and concerns, not corporate platitudes. Communication is so important that you must not pull back from doing it — and a lot of it.

Communicate and Be Visible

Part of working the social side of business is being available to others, so you can help them do their work. This may mean creating easier access to you and even developing an "open door" policy with specific hours when you are available for brief discussions. Be aware of how your verbal and nonverbal communications help or hinder conveying the messages you wish others to receive.

In one company I worked with, the President of one division would stop and chat with people when he went to refill his cup of coffee. Those two-minute interactions with team members inspired and motivated people to action. Similarly, any time you are entering or exiting the building or walking down the halls between meetings is a good time to demonstrate you are present and available. Unfortunately, with today's technology, leaders are looking more at their mobile devices than interacting with the people right in front of them. Be mindful of what you project to others.

- Are you available and open to discussing business?
- What language do you use to convey messages to motivate others to action?
- How does your assistant handle requests for meetings?
- How do you spend your time when visiting company facilities? Are you booked solid in meetings and hastily shuttled from meeting to meeting? Or is there time for people to interact with you?
- Do you make time for customers and suppliers to have meaningful partner discussions? Or do you find that you are only meeting with customers when issues have escalated?

Your transition will set the stage for how people perceive your availability over the long run in your new role. Executive assistants and others who support you will also convey how available, open, and receptive you are to meeting with others. You may not have time to fit in an hour's discussion, but it's wise to clear your calendar so that you can find 15 minutes or so to speak with someone when they request it. When you manage the social and emotional side of the business as well as you do the overall business performance, you will start to see the engagement grow.

Chapter 13

Creating Your Communication Plan

To effectively communicate, we must realize that we are all different in the way we perceive the world and use this understanding as a guide to our communications with others.

— Tony Robbins

In everything you do, work to express yourself to others with meaning and purpose to convey crucial messages consistently and frequently. When communications aren't clear, people spend too much time trying to interpret the messages. This chapter outlines how to communicate clearly and effectively from the start by creating a Transition Communication Plan.

Often, leaders think they are communicating enough— though few actually are. Communication is a core leadership skill that requires constant attention. Effective communications are ones consistently made, then repeated over and over in different formats, so people really hear and take in the messages. Test that these messages are aligned with the business strategy. Ensure that the communications match what is actually happening in the company, so that people don't get confused. Above all, leverage communications to stay visible to your stakeholders.

Your Transition Communication Plan should set out how you plan to be visible throughout your transition and beyond. Your communications are frequently less about what you want to say, and more about what people need to hear. People want to know how your approach will affect their work. They want to know what information they will receive, what's important, and what they should be doing. Creating a Transition Communication Plan will give you an approach to open and then improve the channels of communication.

Create Your Transition Communication Plan

A Transition Communication Plan is part of the Executive Transition Playbook. It creates a structure for your formal and informal discussions and lays out the "who, what, when, where, and how." It sets out a strategy for how you connect with the organization. Because it is your plan, be sure to "own" it. Sometimes, you can work with the organization's Corporate Communications department regarding the writing and distributing of your communications. Even if communications support is available, you should take the lead on the communications' style, form, content, and distribution. Your audiences will be able to tell whether the messages are in your voice. Your communications — and the relationships built through them — are too important to leave to the standard corporate processes.

Communications should be both formal and informal. You need to be in charge of both types of communication, and the style of both should match. How you act, what you say, and your style of talking with others all help people see and understand your personal brand. If you work with Corporate Communications, ask them to help you convey messages in such a way that the messages actually sound like you, in your "voice." When your formal and informal communications match, it helps you build authenticity.

Your communication plan should include: a communications strategy, a set of communications principles, tools for communicating, and plans and timelines for both broad and detailed communications. Incorporate formal as well as informal communications into the plan. Informal ones are more likely to make you visible where and when needed. All communications should be reviewed by you to make sure that the tone, language, and messages match the purposes.

Communicate with a Purpose

Start your communication plan by developing a list of communication principles. These will serve as the foundation for how your messages look, feel, and sound. Such principles help to ensure consistency throughout your transition. Here are some principles you might find useful:

- Communicate messages with conviction, and optimism.
- Use direct conversation whenever possible.
- Be transparent, sharing what is appropriate.
- Start with existing communications tools whenever possible.
- Reinforce the company's values, vision, and strategy.
- Make it clear when you do not know the answer.
- Come to meetings prepared with questions.
- Follow up on action items.
- Determine if messages are received with the appropriate intent.
- Prepare communications well ahead of time.
- Brief senior leaders, direct reports, and peers before important announcements so they are not blindsided.

Encourage Dialogue through Forums

There are many ways to convey messages. We have become used to communicating through emails, short voicemails, texts, and even chat groups, yet sometimes these brief messages can be incomplete or misleading. When communications are not clear, people may create their own meaning, which can lead to misplaced effort, misunderstandings, and incorrect information. Communication can differ by business, and each leader has a preferred style. Figure out how you wish to craft your messages — your full messages — in ways that convey the right information, using an appropriate style that enables people to do their jobs well.

People process and absorb information in different ways and at different speeds. Instead of communicating a message just once, I suggest communicating the same message many times in various ways, using alternate communication vehicles so that your meaning actually gets through. Here are some different types of forums to consider for distributing your messages:

+ Lunch-and-learns
+ Walking the halls
+ Leader forums
+ Social gatherings around a specific business or leadership topic
+ All-employee town hall meetings, which include a discussion format, breakout sessions, and refreshments when appropriate
+ CEO memo with weekly musings, such as "Where in the world is…?" and "Ask me a question"
+ Intranet pages, blogs, microblogs, tweets, and chat rooms
+ Informal breakfast and lunch meetings
+ "Virtual" cup of coffee or lunch discussions (conducted via phone, teleconference, or a corporate chat site)
+ Audiovisual messages and emails or newsletters
+ Quarterly one-on-one meetings with key direct reports of your own direct reports

Use these forums to create a dialogue, rather than a monologue. The best approach is to ask questions and get people talking. Make it acceptable to have a conversation with you. When you are sharing information, tailor your message to your audience. Map out what you want people to know; decide how the message will affect them; consider how you want them to feel afterward. Determine what actions you wish people to take after they fully hear your message.

Chapter 14

Listening: The Art of Engagement

We have two ears and one mouth and we should use them proportionally.

– Susan Cain

Listen, Listen, and Listen Some More

According to Julian Treasure, an expert in listening techniques, we spend roughly 60 percent of our communication time listening, but we retain only about 25 percent of what we hear. He says we are losing our ability to listen. The lack of good listening in business can cause issues to arise when you are trying to build relationships, help others understand business concepts, and lead your fellow workers.

When we actively listen, people feel heard. You create a dialogue and mutual understanding. When you become more conscious about your listening, your understanding and engagement increase significantly.

Unfortunately, listening can be a difficult skill for leaders to learn, since they are accustomed to directing the conversation. Yet, transitions require careful listening. You will be given a lot of information from multiple sources and will need to find a way to sort through it all. You may even have a tendency to filter out messages that do not fit your assumptions. So make every effort to hear messages that disagree with your orientation, as well as those that support your plans.

Listening starts with being able to listen to oneself. When we can take a pause from our busy lives and sit in silence, we can learn to listen to ourselves without judgment or the need to change or fix anything. We are then able to listen to the rest of the world.

Conscious Listening

To bring focus to the topic and give keen attention to the person talking, practice conscious listening. During this process, the listener practices listening without feeling the need to respond. Using conscious listening, the leader can then be present, with attention fully on the speaker. The listener thus creates a safe environment for the speaker to share information.

Conscious listening also allows us to be aware of our thoughts, feelings, and beliefs. It gives us a way to put into perspective the information we receive from others, and to thoughtfully prepare how we share comments and feedback. When we listen consciously, we can gain the benefit of what people are actually trying to communicate. Conscious listening is first about listening and then about absorbing. You can then respond thoughtfully to the speaker.

Leaders can become enamored with their own solutions and shut off input from others. When we believe our ideas are better than those of others, we put ourselves and the business at risk, because we may not be looking objectively at the full situation. Our business judgment can become clouded, and we are apt to make mistakes. Conscious listening can pull us back to the present to hear what is really being said.

Practice Listening

Leaders can become so expert at filtering outside noise that they may actually stop listening to the inputs. Such leaders become deaf to objections, whether stated or hinted at, and search to hear only things that match their own thinking. They can also become impatient with long explanations, if they are accustomed to receiving information only in sound bites. Unless the volume is turned up and conscious listening is a habit, important messages can be missed.

In a July 2011 TED talk, Julian Treasure shared simple practices to improve listening skills:

1. Sit in Silence

Take three minutes every day and sit in silence, with no distractions from digital devices or phones. This helps to reset and recalibrate your hearing, so that you can hear the quiet over the noise.

2. Tune in to the Sound

See if you can separate different sounds, like those of several channels on the radio. Notice whether you can hear and identify the different sounds in a noisy location.

3. Find the Rhythm

Listen to the rhythm of mundane noises, such as the sound of traffic, a clock ticking, water trickling in a fountain, the rebooting of your computer, or the hum of an air conditioner.

4. Become a Better Listener in Conversations

- Receive – Give your full attention to the person talking to you.
- Appreciate – Reinforce others by making small noises ("uh-huh," "I see," "umm").
- Summarize – Paraphrase what you heard back to the speaker to check that you heard the information correctly.
- Ask – Pose questions, both to clarify what you heard and to build on shared ideas.

Chapter 15

Building Rapport with Your Boss

Trust is knowing that when a team member does push you, they're doing it because they care about the team.

– Patrick Lencioni

Find Common Ground

The more senior your position, the more that people will want to be consulted and informed on various facets of the business. While you might be accountable for running the business, there are others who will be affected and wish to have influence over the decisions. They may be your boss, Board members, or investors. They could be customers, employees, or even analysts. Your direct boss is one of many who will want to be engaged. Whomever you report to, take the time to build rapport.

At some point, the conceptual conversations that took place during the interview process change to focus on the true realities of the business. You may be excited about creating a new vision, only to find that your focus is first required on other business needs. You begin to understand the difference between what you thought you were hired to do and what actually needs to be accomplished in the short term. You have a choice: You can push back on the advice and counsel, or you can use your executive presence and gravitas to find a workable solution. Many of my conversations with executives have been to strategize about how the executive works through differences of opinions on running the business.

Usually, when leaders struggle with their relationships with senior managers, no one wins, especially you. The "you versus them" approach just causes unnecessary silos. Everyone is working for the same business, but some may have different perceptions and approaches. Do not expect others to always have the emotional and social intelligence to manage these conversations. It's best for you to have the ability to navigate through challenging discussions and relationships. Everyone wins when you can take the high road and work toward some agreeable solution.

In your senior role, you are bound to view the business differently than others. So find ways to take a full view of the business and see all sides of the issue. Express your ideas in terms that allow others to understand your point of view. Listen to the input of others and be clear on what actions you will take. The various perspectives will enable you and the company to make the best decisions.

Make the most of these discussions and meetings by preparing ahead of time the topics, questions, and key points you wish to cover. The Goals and Business Review One-Pager outlined in Chapter 6 and the Stakeholder Preparation Plan reviewed in Chapter 11 are helpful tools to organize your thoughts and prepare for these important conversations. When you are fully ready for these conversations, you are better positioned to lead the conversation to a better outcome. Save time at the end of the meeting to capture decisions and agree on next steps. Follow the meeting with a short note that captures the ideas and actions.

Chapter 16

Assimilating with Your Management Team

Culture does not change because we desire to change it.
Culture changes when the organization is transformed; the
culture reflects the realities of people working together
every day.

— Frances Hesselbein

It's assumed the team at the top, known as the Executive Team or Senior Management Team, or sometimes the Executive Committee, possesses the team-building and leadership skills to work together. All too often, the reality is that many top teams really struggle to work together. The lack of a high-performing executive team affects how the entire organization works together. If you are fortunate to inherit a high-performing team, your job will be to cultivate the camaraderie.

As the incoming executive, you most likely have your own preconceived notions of how you will lead the team. Those on the team recognize that there will be changes. They will want to hear from you, and will be curious about how you will engage the team. An Assimilation Work Session helps you and your team to get to know one another and determine how to work together. Using an assimilation exercise allows you to assess how the current team works today and where to make changes to create the team you want.

Usually, the Human Resources department — often working with an outside facilitator — runs such an assimilation session, according to its set process and with a goal of meeting the organization's needs.

This doesn't mean, though, that you cannot review the outline of the session ahead of time and make suggestions for additional topics that will help you in your transition.

Figure 16-1 show the steps to prepare for an Assimilation Work Session. The agenda in Figure 16-2 takes you through the activities for the Assimilation Work Session, from premeeting preparation to postmeeting follow-up. This session creates a nonthreatening, productive way to get to know the management team.

Preparing for an Assimilation Work Session   Figure 16-1

Your Actions:

- Meet with the facilitator to discuss the agenda.
- Choose a meeting venue. Make sure it is a place where the participants can fully participate and work without distractions.
- Send the agenda to the participants and introduce the facilitator to them.
- Formulate questions to ask the participants.
- Create a one- to three-page presentation for sharing your background, personal brand, values, and expectations.
- Agree with the facilitator on the interactive fun, exercises, icebreakers, and social activity for the session.

The Facilitator's Actions:

- Meet with the transitioning leader to set an agenda.
- Contact participants to discuss the agenda and the expectations.
- Gather topics and questions for the session.
- Work with the transitioning leader on the interactive fun, exercises, icebreakers, and social activity for the session.

Meeting Objectives:

- Create a safe environment to discuss the opinions on important topics and to alleviate concerns.
- Exchange information in the spirit of learning.

Agenda for an Assimilation Work Session

Figure 16-2

Agenda Item	Outcomes
Meeting Agenda and Expectations	◆ Gain clarity and alignment on what the meeting will cover.
Discuss Meeting Agreements	◆ Develop meeting agreements to create a safe environment. ◆ Agree on confidentiality to encourage open and candid dialogue.
Leader Opening Comments	◆ Share leadership background and insights.
Question Generation Brainstorm	Leader's questions brainstorm: ◆ Develop questions to ask the participants. Participants' questions brainstorm (led by facilitator): ◆ Generate questions and items to ask the new leader. ◆ Topics may include: personal style, approach to business, communications, problem-solving, decision-making style, teamwork, performance expectations, priorities, planned changes, impact of changes. ◆ Prioritize and create common themes. ◆ Determine how questions will be shared with the leader.
Main Session: Question Discussion	Participants and leader share the questions.
Framing Responses	Provide time for participants and leader to prepare answers.
Main Session: Sharing the Responses	Participants and leader share responses to the questions and engage in discussion.
Go-Forward Plans	Discuss agreements. Decide on management processes. Outline accountabilities.
Actions and Next Steps	Discuss actions and next steps.
Communications and Closing Remarks	◆ Identify what will be communicated to those in the organization who weren't in this session. ◆ Leader makes any closing comments.
Team Activity	Include a team-building activity in the session to promote connection.
Postmeeting Follow-Up	Articulate communication action items, team agreements, and management processes.

The result of the Assimilation Work Session should be an understanding among all parties about one another and about how everybody will work together to meet organizational goals. The session also provides an opportunity for you to assess the people on your team. It is important for your own success to have the right people in the right roles. These sessions will help you evaluate the thinking, style, and effectiveness of the participants. The discussions that arise will shape your ideas about how to align your strategy, processes, and people.

Figure 16-3 suggests an outline of the information you will want to share about yourself with the other participants in the Assimilation Work Session. Chapter 8 reviews more details on how to create and communicate your personal brand and other messages about your background and expectations.

Outline for a Leader's Introduction Presentation   Figure 16-3

1. **My goals and objectives in the first three months**

2. **A bit about me**
   - Who I am — my personal brand. What's important to me?
   - What do I love to do when I'm not working?
   - What would people say about me?
   - What are my core leadership values?
   - How do I like to work?

3. **Working together during this transition**
   - What can you expect from me?
   - What can I reasonably ask of you?

Before you move on from this exercise, take a few minutes to capture your personal observations of the overall team, as well as of the individuals on the team. Figure 16-4 shows a simple Team Member Assessment template. This template will come in handy as you assess the team and its members' individual capabilities.

Even though this session may be designed and run by others, you can exert significant influence on the information covered in it.

Team Member Assessment		Figure 16-4
Name/Role	Initial Impressions	Actions/Next Steps

Chapter 17

Making the Most of Meetings with Direct Reports

You cannot push anyone up the ladder unless he is willing to climb.

– Andrew Carnegie

Prepare for One-on-One Conversations with Direct Reports

One-on-one conversations provide an excellent forum for getting to know individuals and their contributions to the business. These meetings can offer you a way to hear about the company through different individuals' perspectives as well as a way to assess the capabilities and talents currently in the organization. You will want to couple these one-on-one conversations with group discussions. Come into these meetings with a focus on listening and learning how you can best serve the business versus what you can do to fix, change, or adjust the organization. Stating your intention of giving real service will allow you to listen more deeply, rather than simply feeling a need to react on the spot to the information that will be shared.

While you are assessing the people and the business itself, your direct reports will be interested to learn how you will help, or hinder, their careers and work. They will want to know how you work and what they can expect. They especially want to find out your impressions of them, and they will be assessing whether they should stay or leave. This is a "dance of engagement" between you and your direct reports. Leaders who view this engagement as only a one-way street lose the opportunity to hear others' perspectives, step into others' shoes, and understand what their people need to hear.

Prepare for these conversations and create a list of questions. Determine ahead of time which personal and professional stories you will share, then map out a series of interactions and conversations. If the organizational culture supports it, I suggest that you start with personal conversations that can then lead up to professional ones.

On the following pages are three suggested outlines for meetings held one on one with your direct reports that should lead to trusted working relationships. I share these outlines so that you can avoid common complaints from direct reports. After such meetings, some will say their new leader wasn't prepared for the early conversations. Others will think the leader jumps too quickly to conclusions, while others will say the new leader spent too much time talking about herself. The point is to make a good first impression, in order to forge a trusting relationship.

Treat your direct reports as you would treat your valued customers. Customer visits usually entail preparation. So create a strategy and plan for the series of conversations with direct reports and other key stakeholders. The first meeting is intended to establish an interpersonal relationship. The second is for discussing the business. The third is for doing a deeper dive into the business. (Of course, you can change this structure to fit the business situation.)

Meeting 1: Getting Acquainted

The first meeting with a direct report is about getting to know each other on a personal level. The best thing is to schedule the first meeting in a neutral location, preferably not your offices but somewhere you can have a casual, uninterrupted conversation. Direct reports will be listening to find out if you are someone they want to follow, or if their job might be in jeopardy. Be curious and interested. Ask questions, and really listen.

While you want to put the direct reports at ease, be careful not to make any promises or commitments you can't keep. Above all, be yourself. Demonstrate your values and behaviors.

Keep the conversation as informal as possible. Some individuals may feel a bit uncomfortable, so work to put them at ease. Ask plenty of open-ended questions to get them talking about themselves. This informal conversation will likely lead to a discussion about their roles, accomplishments, and business interests. Use this time to assess whether each person would be a valuable member of your team.

Try posing these types of questions at this first meeting:

- Tell me about your work and your role. What skills do you bring to your role?
- What are the most rewarding aspects of your job?
- Why do you do your job, besides for the paycheck?
- How can I support you?
- What brings out the best in you? What are your work preferences and styles?
- How would you describe the business and what's working or not working?
- What are you most proud of in this past year? Why?
- What do you like to do when you're not working?
- If you could make a request of anyone in the company, what would you ask for? Why?

You can help your direct reports prepare for this meeting. I suggest sending a short agenda or set of objectives for the meeting. Because they will assume you are reviewing their career and performance, they too will want to be prepared for this important discussion. Consider these possible thought-provoking topics for the agenda:

- What I would like my new leader to know about me is…
- I would describe my own leadership style as…
- What excites me most about my role is…
- My single greatest concern is…
- The two things that would help us be more successful are…
- To get the most out of my performance, it helps to…
- The most effective way to give me feedback is…
- What requires our immediate attention is…
- I consider your top three priorities to be…
- My personal priorities and goals are…

Direct reports will be assessing you, as well. Be prepared to answer questions from them. The most likely ones are:

- Why are you here?
- What is your experience with this industry, this business, and these products?
- What are your plans to…?
- What is your impression of our product or service mix?
- What changes do you intend to make?
- What can I expect?
- What is the best way to work with you?

Some unspoken questions could be: "Are you really as good as people say you are?" Or "Can you really help us improve our business performance?" Or "You're the fifth leader in five years — how long will you be around, and can you make a significant contribution in that time period?"

While you can't change the past, you can have a great impact on the present. Your actions and ability to help others focus will aid in getting the work done.

Leave enough time to share ideas and get all questions answered. Save a few minutes at the end to wrap up the discussion and set the next steps. Do not end the meeting abruptly; the direct reports will take that as a negative sign.

Follow up after each meeting with a short email or note with further comments and suggested actions. People will appreciate this extra effort.

Meeting 2: Discussing the Business

Use this second meeting to talk about the business. Tailor each discussion to match each direct report's roles. Ask open-ended questions, and stay in learning mode. This is a good time to listen carefully and stay present. Try not to interrupt in an attempt to move things along. You can learn a lot about what each person does and how the organization really works when you let the discussion unfold naturally.

Discuss the following topics to help you learn how the organization works:

Business Performance – Objectives, Goals, Strategies, Tactics, Financials

People and Team – How are things working in your area? How do we engage our people? Who are our high performers? What is the level of engagement?

Customers – What do customers say about our products? What challenges are we facing in the market?

Vendors and Partnerships – What is our strategy with working with others? Who are considered strategic partners?

Working Together – Roles and Expectations

Processes – How are the processes enabling or hindering work outputs?

Enterprise Initiatives – Which are we planning?

Working across the Organization – How do you and your team work with other areas?

Opportunities and Challenges – Give examples.

Support – What support do you need from me, and what other resource requirements do you have?

Professional Career Development – What are your career aspirations?

Miscellaneous – What other advice do you have as we move forward?

You may not have time to fully cover all these topics during this second meeting. What you are looking to do is get a high-level overview that will enable you to delve into more-detailed discussions in future meetings.

To minimize the time that people need to prepare for these one-on-one meetings, ask your direct reports to use only existing documents for your review. The key is to have the high-level business conversation with your direct reports. This way, you will learn about the business and observe how your direct reports work. With this information, you will have a better idea about what you want them to keep doing as well as how to shape the process to meet the needs of both of you.

Meeting 3: Performing a Deep-Dive Business Review

By the time you hold the third one-on-one meeting with a direct report, you are getting familiar enough with the business that you can make intelligent comments and ask thought-provoking questions. It will be natural, then, to begin to move into a routine business interaction. Some of your direct reports will look to you for guidance on, decisions about, or confirmation of what they are doing. It is important for you to stay in learning mode and be clear about what you can commit to now, or what you need to follow up on later.

You have come too far in your business analysis not to spend one more meeting further assessing the business. It's best to remind yourself to maintain a broad organizational view and not react to people's functions or business interests. Use this meeting as an opportunity to both dive deeper and look for cross-organizational alignment and interdependencies. When you move into the Assessment and Sharing phases of the Executive Transition Playbook, in Chapters 23 and 24, you will have time to share cohesive next steps.

By this stage, you should have established a cadence and rhythm with your direct reports. You now know far more about how the business operates. Now, you are looking for clear, candid insights about the business's challenges and opportunities. You can ask direct reports for further information about issues, disconnects, and solutions tried in the past. Stay objective, without letting your own opinions leak into the conversation. Until you have fully assessed the entire business, much of what you say may be conjecture and may even fuel rumors or miscommunications about what will happen.

It might be a good idea in this session to let your direct report know that you are taking a "deep dive" into the details and that this won't be your normal way of operating. Your transparency may put people at ease and allow the two of you to use this session for what it is intended: for your learning and education about the business.

Remember: As you share ideas, it can be easy to slip into the mode of talking about how you did things in the past. Instead, ask thought-provoking questions. You can share your ideas without needing to validate these ideas in terms of your former company. By your third meeting, you may find yourself slipping into former ways of working, which may not be appropriate in this role. Focus instead on using the leadership styles and behaviors appropriate both to what you are learning and to the business situation at hand.

In this discussion, you will want to validate and confirm what you know about the business, as well as seek input from your leaders on next steps. This is a time to stay in active listening mode and come prepared with probing questions. Be sure to allow time for people to answer the questions fully. Discussion topics for the third meeting can include a deeper dive from the second meeting, as well as the following:

- Continued discussion of the business and topics raised in Meeting 2
- Key initiatives in which the direct reports are involved
- Opportunities and challenges for all parties
- Risks that the company faces
- Resource requirements
- Process or system requirements
- Talent review

This chapter outlined a series of one-on-one meetings. To build on the data and insights gleaned from them, you will want to create a series of business team review meetings to gain information from the entire team. Use your one-on-one meetings to prepare for the team meetings.

Chapter 18

Finding the Right Talent

Leadership: The art of getting someone else to do
something you want done because he wants to do it.

– Dwight D. Eisenhower

Shape the Executive Team

Getting the right people into the right roles doing the right things takes keen observation and assessment. It requires assessing whether the team of leaders can work together to solve problems and advance the business strategy. Of course, you want the best talent you can find and afford. However, keep in mind that a group of brilliant individuals who can't work together can be worse than a group of mediocre players who complement each other and make up for each other's weak spots.

In essence, you are creating your "A" team, the best team you can assemble. A key activity during your transition is assessing the current team members and determining the best group of individuals to create a high-performing team. This requires getting to know the business, the people, and their skills. Based on the vision and strategy, what is the optimal combination of people to work with you to make the vision a reality? Your job is to find people capable of working with a diversity of people, ideas, and situations. Additionally, you will want individuals who have the breadth and depth to be able to grow with the business. Consider the interpersonal capabilities of others, as this is important when implementing enterprise solutions.

Your boss, or the Board, may ask you to explain your choices, so be prepared to articulate why each person is on the team. Expect others to provide input on the talent decisions you want to make. This exercise may take considerably longer than you planned.

As you are looking at the team composition, also delve several layers into the organization to see if the talent exists. If it doesn't, the organization will struggle when trying to implement initiatives.

You may have to make some tough choices about people that will require you to handle situations with care and compassion. You will need to determine whether you can develop the skills you need from within the organization or whether you must recruit outside talent. You will want to set everyone up for success, whether or not they remain on the team. Others will be watching how you act and will project how you might handle other personnel changes.

Find Your Chief Lieutenants

A leader's role, whether that of a CEO or an Army Chief of Staff, can be very isolating. The key people you worked with in your previous job are no longer around. You need to find new individuals you can count on. Your predecessor likely had a group of internal and external advisors. So take the time in your transition period to determine whether you can, or want to, depend on the same people. Know the type of person you want to surround yourself with, and try to create a balanced group of voices.

Leaders often rely on their Financial, Human Resources, or Marketing executives. Be on the lookout for the people you can count on to be your "chief lieutenants" — the people who will work alongside you and help you formulate business options. Seek out people who will share the unvarnished reality with you, and will help you build collaboration. Additionally, this is a good time to search for high-performing associates who may be able to take on additional projects.

Build Trust

In the early days of your transition, people will be assessing whether they can trust you. Your actions will be a key indicator. Get very clear on what's important to you and how you work with others.

Observing the organization's culture will give you clues about the level of trust that exists. Consider simple things, like: How does information get shared? How are people kept in the loop? Do leaders actually do what they say they will do? What happens when someone makes a mistake? How are interpersonal differences handled? You'll soon find out that when people in a company at all levels have high trust and respect for one another, it becomes easier to discuss problems up and down the chain of command. When trust is low, people spend too much time blaming, defending, and even avoiding one another.

Create a Sustainable Organization

It's never too early to start looking at succession planning, by understanding and making note of the depth of talent in the organization. The last thing you want is to implement an initiative only to find out that the organization lacks the talent and capability to implement it. Start by understanding the talent management process. What are the core competencies for success? How is the talent management process used to find, develop, and manage the talent?

If you were hired from the outside, there will likely be some talent gaps and positions to fill before you can build a solid succession plan. A strong talent bench provides an organization with the resources to take on many initiatives that will grow the company. Speak with Human Resources heads and various business leaders about the current talent in the company and the organization's plans to cultivate and retain talented individuals. Engage such leaders in working with you on a talent management strategy. If you aren't fortunate to have strong Human Resources department capabilities, it might make sense to engage an outside firm to help you set up the appropriate systems, so that your talent strategy matches your business strategy. Both are critical for accomplishing your business goals.

PART IV

Managing Effectively through the Transition

Chapter 19

Keeping the Business on Track

Surround yourself with the strongest, most knowledgeable people, and give them room to express themselves.

— Phil Jackson

Focus on What Matters

In today's work environment, outgoing leaders usually want to move on to their next assignments. You may not get the full attention from them that you need as you move into your new role.

While the first few months in a new position are a time to learn, there most likely will be urgent business issues that require direction and decisions. There may even be a fair amount of pressure from the Board or management to make decisions early in the transition. Some people, while not close to the problem, may believe they know enough about the issue and may press you hard to make a decision. There could be personal agendas creating hype to take action. Your job, whatever the case, is to find a process to make an informed decision even though you are not fully up-to-speed.

How do you keep the business on track and still give yourself some leeway so that you can minimize making fatal errors? Start by recognizing that you may make some mistakes early on that later you will wish you had avoided. Of course, it's easy to look back over a year with more experience and information and be able to see a better path.

The best plan of action is to establish a simple process for addressing key decisions that must be made before you have all the information. You will want to rely on other leaders and trusted advisors to make sure that you and the organization have a full view of the situation. This may mean asking people who are closer to the problem to take the lead in crafting a solution. If there are items that need your immediate attention, create a plan for how you will get involved. Be clear about what you will do and how you will stay on top of the situation. A simple process may look like the following:

- Name the two or three things that need your attention in the next three months.
- Identify what it will take to keep the business on track while giving yourself a chance to learn.
- Name someone you can rely on to oversee the initiative in the interim.
- Define your role in these discussions.
- Outline how decisions will be made and how you will be involved in the decision.
- Schedule periodic check-ins to see how things are progressing.
- Transition leadership oversight to yourself, when appropriate.

It may initially feel good to be active in the business, but remember that you still may not have a complete picture of the situation. Hold off on the temptation to jump in and make decisions without knowing all the facts. You might find that people are afraid to warn you that your early ideas and decisions will take the business off track. My best advice is: Unless it is mission-critical to make a decision, use at least the first month to listen and learn. In the entire transition period, however long it runs, be clear about how you want to be engaged in decisions, as your involvement will likely be different when you step fully into the role.

Be extra-considerate in meetings. Know when it's appropriate to ask questions to deepen your learning and when you are derailing the meeting. It's better to write down questions and observations for follow-up after the meeting than just to extemporize about them on the spot and later be proved wrong.

Recognize when it is better to let the organization operate without you for a certain time. One large organization I consulted with insists that its incoming executives go through an extended onboarding process to learn. The daily leadership is assigned to someone else, so the new executive has ample time to learn about the business, products, culture, and markets. This company has found that the assimilation and success rates of entering executives have increased dramatically. In your case, while others may make the top-level decisions during your first few months, you will want to take full accountability for those decisions when you are finally ready to assume the role.

Chapter 20

Leading in the New Organization

Be yourself; everyone else is already taken.

– Oscar Wilde

Stay Engaged as You Move Farther Away from the Action

With every move you make up the corporate ladder, you actually get one step farther away from the company's day-to-day activities. You may have anticipated more control over decision-making, yet feel powerless about it. So take care that the messages you and others send do not get lost in translation. Strike a balance of working at the enterprise level and creating the forums that enable you to engage in more detailed discussions without overstepping your role. This will give you a clearer picture of the business.

Inspire two-way dialogue and idea exchanges by incorporating work sessions within the business reviews. Far too often, business reviews become one-way presentations, with so many topics being crammed into the session that little time remains for discussion. Leave enough time for a working session that engages the group, versus having the usual old report-out sessions. Keep the conversation active by briefing other senior leaders and your direct reports in advance on how you'd like them to participate in these sessions. Then your executive briefing sessions will be transformed into work sessions. The executive team will move from merely looking for problems to cultivating a multilayer conversation that can analyze and then actually solve problems. Bringing yourself closer to the action in a coaching and consultative role allows you to tap the organization's layers of talent for unique solutions and ideas.

Not Wrong, Just Different

It's easy to fall into the trap of seeing what's not working and focusing on how to fix it, instead of seeing what's working that can be built on. As you look at the business, you will find many differences from your own approach. You may need to reframe your viewpoint to see these differences as opportunities, instead of dismissing them as "wrong." If you find yourself criticizing the business aloud to your colleagues, reframe your comments to be more productive. Balance your views and share what's working as well as what needs to be changed. Too much constructive feedback can feel like criticism if it's not delivered properly. The intent is to find the best solutions, not to disenfranchise those who do the real work.

How you look at diverse ideas and concepts will shape how your fellow leaders approach differences. Encourage people to use the diversity of thinking to their advantage. Find ways to stimulate creativity so that it's acceptable to voice different opinions before converging on a workable solution. Pay tribute to and leverage the strengths of the organization to build a solid foundation for the future.

It's up to you, as the new leader, to create a safe environment for people to share ideas and give direct leadership feedback to you. People will want to follow you if you can demonstrate credibility and value. As people see they can count on you, trust builds. Your encouragement to surface different ideas and opinions will open the opportunity for growth.

Attend to the Emotional Side of Business

In any transition, there is a tendency to focus on the technical preparation and to find that managing the business is actually the easy part. Myriad challenges can lie in the personal and interpersonal elements of the new role. For instance, you might find yourself spending more time with the Board, handling sensitive matters. Perhaps you realize it takes many individual conversations to socialize an idea before people are ready to discuss the topic in a larger group. Maybe you are expected to commit significant blocks of time to executive forums with your peers. You might not feel that some of these discussions are necessary or even relevant.

You may need to make some adjustments to work in this new way. Some say the "soft" stuff becomes the "hard" stuff in these new roles. Taking the time to understand the additional demands on your time and how you will handle the interpersonal interactions will help you and others work toward a common goal.

When you are able to observe yourself and become aware of how your own beliefs and natural reactions shape your actions, you can choose ways in which you want to act. Use your transition to become aware of your personal points of view and of how your beliefs affect your actions. Cultivate the social intelligence to understand and learn from others' perspective. Listen to a diversity of ideas and come up with the best possible solutions. Use these insights to convey messages in ways others can hear and act on them.

With emotional and social awareness, you will be able to bring your authentic self into your work. When you listen and observe, you become better able to communicate clearly in a way others can hear and act on.

Your new role will likely require you to develop new behaviors that enhance your emotional and social awareness. Building this awareness helps leaders to effectively lead both themselves and others through even the most challenging of times.

Create Dialogue

Some leaders may find it easier to "tell" people what to do to get the work completed. Unfortunately, "telling" people to do something does not necessarily mean that they will carry out the request or will execute the work in the way you want it done. People may need more dialogue or specifics to get the work started. They may want to be included in the decisions as well as to be a part of the solution. This may require looking at the issues from all sides and soliciting ongoing feedback to keep things moving along.

It's amazing how people can get stuck when looking at a problem from only one angle. The best way to keep people working on the right things is to develop a dialogue and exchange of ideas. This goes beyond restating the problem. Look below the surface to find out what's hindering progress, then remove any obstacles in the way.

The feedback you share can help others see a broader perspective and look beyond the obvious issues. Sometimes people have to see what is working in order to pave the path to find the full solution. So pay attention to how your comments increase dialogue, or how perhaps they silence the room, then look for ways to get people talking. As you cultivate the conversation, sit back and listen. These discussions can provide valuable input for you to coach and mentor others. The group will be more productive when you move from stiff, executive briefing sessions in which people are afraid to talk to open-dialogue sessions where everyone becomes an integral part of shaping the solution.

Work in a New Way

When you move into a new role — especially one at a higher level — you may find that you need to adjust your leadership style to fit the situation. Pick and choose thoughtfully how and when you assert authority and otherwise carry out the functions of the new role. What you say and how you convey the message — including your nonverbal behaviors — can increase (or lessen) the probability of engaging others.

Frequently, a new role involves expanding your responsibilities and scope of leadership. If you listen and learn in your transition period, you should gain insights into how you may have to adjust your current business and leadership behaviors. Learning how to be a coach and a mentor to others can open the door to richer conversations.

Traps and Tips You May Face in Your New Role   Figure 20-1

TRAPS	TIPS
Working at a level below the new role.	Elevate your leadership behaviors.
Doing the work of others versus coaching.	Delegate activities that others can do.
Telling people what to do versus encouraging them to action.	Get others engaged in the solution.
Being unavailable to others and difficult to schedule a meeting with them.	Be visible and accessible so that you can shape concepts and ideas.
Criticizing the prior work.	Build on what's working.
Focusing more on activities and "doing" versus setting a strategic direction.	Know when to drill down into details and when to be more strategic and higher-level.
Requesting that reports be formatted the way you prefer.	Review current reports and processes before making changes.
Letting yourself get isolated from the conversations.	Recognize you don't know what you don't know, ask questions, and listen.

Through a coaching approach, people see you as someone who is helping guide the discussions, instead of simply stepping in and taking over.

Every step into a more senior position requires new behaviors. Often, leaders get stuck working in old ways. Figure 20-1 shows some traps you may face as well as tips for avoiding those traps as you enter a new role.

You have probably heard the saying, "What got you here may not get you to where you want to go." Most likely, your new assignment requires different actions than the ones in your previous assignment. Review your personal SWOT analysis from Chapter 7 in the context of the new business situation to determine what you need to stop doing, what you should start doing, and what you should continue doing to enable your success.

As you move up the leadership ladder, you may find the shifts in your behavior to be more subtle than they were earlier in your career. Critically examine your new role and the business situation to assess what skills you need for success. Then create a Leadership Plan to develop those skills. Be sure to look at both the technical and the interpersonal skills required.

Make a list of the areas you need to address, then determine what changes you must make to act as a leader in this new role. Review the Leadership Plan Worksheet you created in Figure 7-2 to look at common areas to address in your Leadership Plan. Keep this simple; in each area, identify the one or two top-priority actions. This will make it easy to apply them in your daily routine. Once the new behaviors become a habit, choose additional leadership behaviors to develop, again a few at a time.

It can be helpful to get feedback as soon as you start your new behaviors. Ask trusted colleagues to observe these behaviors in meetings and give you their thoughts on how you are doing. Consider testing your leadership effectiveness by asking for 360-degree feedback after your first six to eight months in the role. This can provide valuable information for making any necessary adjustments so that you can better serve others in the company.

The Essential Skill of Giving and Receiving Feedback

Your transition is a time for inquiry and exploration. It requires you and others to make adjustments and learn how to work with each other. You will be giving others feedback, and receiving it in one form or another from your stakeholders. Knowing how to give and receive feedback becomes an essential leadership skill.

Always consider your tone, words, and comments whenever you communicate with others. Observe how you share ideas, so that you come across as sincere and caring, with the intent to help, not harm. Whenever you provide feedback, take care to make your messages objective, fact-based, and clear. See if you can observe the impact your comments have on others. Reinforce the desired behaviors with positive feedback, not negative comments. Instead of criticizing and finding fault, frame your comments to create a learning environment so that others can take positive actions to improve.

Pay attention to how you yourself receive feedback. Create a safe environment so people feel comfortable sharing their insights with you. You may need to assist others who may be uncomfortable giving feedback. When you are receiving feedback, actively listen, without emotion, to the ideas the person is sharing. It's easy to deflect or make light of positive feedback instead of listening and acknowledging the input. Also, try not to get defensive or push back against what is being said when it feels like criticism. People may not be aware of how they are coming across. Rather, allow them to show you different options and courses of action. Then, demonstrate that you have heard the feedback by paraphrasing their remarks, and finally thank them for their honesty and insights.

One final thought on feedback: Most people will avoid sharing bad news, as they are afraid the leader will blame the messenger. If you do not know the issues, you cannot be part of the solution; therefore, reinforce others for providing both "good" and "bad" news. One executive I worked with learned to listen to the full message about a problem before providing a thoughtful reply. He was careful not to accuse or criticize. He realized this news was a gift that could help the organization improve.

How you handle issues, over time, in your new role will reflect on how much information is shared with you. When people recognize that you will listen without "killing the messenger," more opportunities for improvements will surface. While you will want to support the identification of problems, you will also want to encourage others to find creative solutions. As you promote the delivery of both "good" and "bad" news, you will be able to facilitate richer discussions.

Chapter 21

Organizing Information

Organizing is what you do before you do something so that when you do it, it is not all mixed up.

– A. A. Milne

Create an Executive Transition Sourcebook

As you move through your transition, you are gathering significant amounts of information. It can be helpful to set up a system to collect and organize the information for easy reference and review. I recommend that you develop an Executive Transition Sourcebook with various sections, including tabs for business, people, processes, leadership, communication, and external constituents, plus any others that will help you. Figure 21-1 shows a possible outline for the sections in an Executive Transition Sourcebook. This Sourcebook can keep all your key insights and information in an organized place that will be extremely useful when you conduct business briefings with the Board and senior management. It's a valuable tool that will help you analyze the business at many levels and then develop your own strategy for improvements and for your go-forward plans.

In the Sourcebook you will collect enterprise, business unit, geographical, and functional information in one place. This may include presentations, financials, plans, processes, and many other documents. Use Figure 9-2, Business Ecosystem Considerations, outlined in Chapter 9, as a guide to collecting information. Depending on the business, it may be a good idea to create separate Sourcebook sections to let you look at the entire business, as well as the business units, divisions, functions, regions, and even countries if yours is a global business.

Executive Transition Sourcebook

Figure 21-1

Tabs	Content for Each Sourcebook Tab

The Business

Enterprise Mission, Vision, Values
Financials (Historical & Current)
Objectives, Goals, Scorecards,
   Dashboards
Strategic Operating Plans
Key Initiatives

Business Challenges/Gaps in Plan
Brands/Products
Divisions/Business Segments
Functions (Finance, Marketing,
   Sales, Operations, HR, R&D)
Geographic Regions/Countries

Process/Systems

Operating Model & Management
   Processes
Corporate Calendar
Annual Planning Process

Core Operating Processes
Supply/Demand Forecasting
New Product Development Process
Business Development Process
IT System/Operating Platforms

People & Organization

Organizational Structure
Strategic Talent Management
  ♦ Talent Strategy
  ♦ Compensation & Benefits
  ♦ Performance Appraisal System

♦ Succession Planning
♦ Learning & Development Plans
♦ Cultural Assessment
♦ Recruiting Schedule
♦ Leadership Capability Review

Leadership

Direct Reports & Performance
   Reviews
Executive Management Team –
   Assimilation Work Session

My Personal Leadership
♦ Executive Transition Playbook
♦ Leadership Plan
♦ Healthy Daily Practices

Communications

Communication Principles

Communication Strategy

Communication Plan & Timeline

External Constituents

Board of Directors
Customers, Markets, Consumers,
   Communities
Suppliers, Vendors, Partnerships
Investors, Shareholders

Competitors
Government Officials, Regulatory
   Agencies
Financial Institutions
Professional Organizations & Trade
   Associations

Gather the insights you have gained through your learning so that you can take an objective, holistic look at what you've discovered. Add your personal insights to the appropriate sections of the Sourcebook. Then review the information and draw your conclusions about what actions to take.

With information coming in daily from many directions and different areas, you may find it best to gather the information into the sections on a weekly basis. When the pertinent information is in one place, it's easy to have it handy for reference. As you review the information, what do you see as common and similar themes across the business? Where do the differences occur? For instance, is there a good reason for certain business segments being operated differently, or does that indicate a lack of strategic alignment that should be addressed?

Use the information to identify the core themes. Look for interdependencies across the business. Laying out the information so that you can see the entire business ecosystem will show you the strengths and weaknesses throughout the business. It will provide a visual map for determining the implications of changing one aspect of the business and the ramifications of that on other areas. Collecting the information in one place allows you to sequence the business priorities, tag interdependencies, and share your ideas with others. The Sourcebook offers an enterprise view from which to identify next steps.

Chapter 22

Cultivating Relationships

Trust is the glue in relationships and organizations.

— Stephen Covey

Stay Connected

I can't emphasize strongly enough how important it is that you cultivate networks inside and outside the company, as well as keep in periodic contact with the network of people who can support you. Take a chapter out of Dale Carnegie's classic *How to Make Friends and Influence People* to cultivate thought-provoking relationships with a wide variety of constituents.

Relationships are built on communication. It's a continuous learning process to be aware of how you are communicating your intentions, and how your language, tone, and tenor either connect with or disengage from those with whom you come in contact. Each stakeholder will need different things from you. Anticipating those needs makes your job easier. It won't all be about business. People will also want to relate to you as a person. In some of your circles, the personal discussions are as important as the business content.

With so many people wanting to engage with you, why is it so easy to get isolated in your new role? You should ask yourself what you could be doing that contributes to this isolation. For one thing, the pulls of the job get in the way. For example, you promised to get back in touch with a colleague after a terrific interaction, but find there's no time in your schedule for the next few months. And if your executive assistant tries to protect your schedule, the message gets out that you may not be approachable. Your genuine desire to help on an issue turns into a monologue of you "telling" others your views, without giving them the opportunity to comment. In fact, your comments may sound more like criticism than helpful solutions.

To stay in touch effectively with others, you need to actively manage your relationships. Keep a list of the people you want to stay in touch with, and indicate on the list how often you'd like to make a connection. Put dates in your calendar or planner. Personalize the Example of a Stakeholder Preparation Plan (Figure 11-1) to prepare for key discussions.

Make a real difference in your follow-up. Carry note cards so that you can send handwritten notes of praise or insight or simple appreciation to high-performing associates. You will stand out, as few people send pen-and-ink handwritten notes these days. The personal touch definitely makes a difference.

Avoid Becoming Isolated

As an enterprise leader, you have the advantage of seeing the entire business landscape. At the same time, you may be too far away and isolated from the real work activity to have a true impact. Unless you are careful, most of the information you hear will be sound bites and headlines that have been censored and filtered by your direct reports. The more layers there are in your organization, the more likely it is that the information you receive is synthesized and possibly slanted by others (or just plain wrong).

Use your unique position to help make the cross-organizational connections and help leaders see the full business picture so that they can collectively find the best solution. Work to break through the barriers and silos by creating forums to talk directly to people and share information. Get involved and actively engage with a cross section of the organization to avoid getting isolated.

Cultivating relationships and assessing the talent can go hand in hand. Look several layers deep inside the organization to meet the rising leaders. Solicit their perspective on the business, and learn about what's keeping them motivated and what's challenging them. The more you delve into the entire organization, the more you will see the day-to-day realities of how senior management decisions are truly playing out throughout the organization, for good or ill.

In talking with people at various levels, you will see how messages and direction move from your direct reports down to the front line. This is valuable information for you, so meet and get to know people at all levels and ask them to share their ideas and perspectives regarding the business. Consider setting up ongoing forums to connect with multiple levels in the organization, so that you can hear and see for yourself what's really going on.

Develop Strong Peer Relationships

Many say that strong bonds with peers are the most important relationships to cultivate. It's easy to get a false sense that your efforts are working with direct reports, since you are in a position of authority and they likely look up to you. Not so with peers. You may find you need to shift your approach somewhat to gain their respect.

Pave the way for cross-organizational collaboration by engaging with your peer group. Peers will have their own views, opinions, and approaches, and may not readily agree with your ideas. Your time will be well spent in building collaboration and cooperation among your peers. Prepare for meetings with them by using the Stakeholder Preparation Plan discussed in Chapter 11. Include both peers with whom you naturally connect well and those whom you may need to work a bit harder to reach. Use your meeting time to review business items and to find ways to enhance the business.

Try several techniques to develop stronger relationships with your peers, and regularly assess their effectiveness:

Connect on a Personal Level

Go beyond the business meetings and get to know your peers. This may include talking more on a personal level and getting to know one another over a lunch discussion or even a weekend golf game or boating trip. Be prepared to listen to what your peers view as important.

Collaborate Well

Be curious and ask questions. As you hear different ideas and approaches, take care not to dismiss your peers' ideas too quickly. Discuss ways in which you can mutually support one another's business efforts. People will take notice when they see you working to mutually solve issues that cut across your organization.

Provide Mutual Support

Volunteer to help your peers, and in turn ask for assistance from them.

Build Trust

Relationships are constructed on trust. Take the time to set expectations of how you will work together. Share information and work toward solutions that benefit the entire organization. Regularly ask colleagues for feedback, to learn how you can better contribute to the management team.

You and your peer group will want to show a united front in supporting the business initiatives. A trap that many new leaders fall into is to approach a problem too myopically instead of considering the broader implications across the entire business ecosystem. As you and your colleagues work on initiatives, take care that you do not solve one problem only to find that you have created another one. This can happen when a business fails to take a true ecosystem approach.

PART V

Leading Effectively for the Long Term

Chapter 23

Assessing and Using the Information Collected

The first step toward change is awareness.

– Nathaniel Branden

If you have taken the time to collate an Executive Transition Sourcebook, you can use the information in it to identify key business themes and make pertinent decisions. Otherwise, this is a good time to collect the pertinent information in one place before turning your attention to step 3 of the Executive Transition Playbook: Assess the Business.

Your assessment will produce a clear picture of the business and what to do next. Use the assessment period to collect your thoughts, weigh the options, and get clear on next steps. How is the business performing today, and where do you want to make changes? Make notes on how the organization will react to any changes you will be proposing. Here is where the clarity of messages becomes important, enabling you to adequately address the questions and concerns and to build buy-in. The key is to create a direction where you wish to take the business. With a clear picture of what needs to be accomplished, map out how you will socialize and then enroll others in your campaign.

The following ideas are meant to spark your thinking about next steps for the overall strategy, leadership capabilities, and business implementation. Depending on your situation, you may find that you need to address other aspects of the business, such as organizational structure, processes, or perhaps metrics. You will likely want to dig deeper into specific tools to address these areas. The key is to clarify the themes and share them with other leaders and, together, get the organization focusing on next steps.

Chart a Direction

Refer back to the information you've captured about the business. Take a look at the strategy of the business and assess how well the organization is following it, in light of these questions:

- Is the organization working in concert with the company's mission, vision, and values? Are leaders committed and aligned to the company's vision, values, and strategy?
- Is the company well positioned and valued by customers, strategic suppliers, and competitors?
- Is the strategy clearly defined? Is it achieving the desired results?
- Do business segments, functions, and departments themselves have clearly defined strategies? Are those strategies aligned to the enterprise strategy?
- Are work processes clearly defined? Do people follow them, or do they create work-arounds?
- Are people engaged and concentrating on the right things?
- How aligned are the work efforts across the organization?
- What themes are emerging?

It's one thing to have a strategy; it's another to follow its direction. Check to see if people are truly committed to the strategic direction. If they are not, what are they spending their time on, and why?

When business units and functional departments become more focused on activities and dealing with the day-to-day issues, the strategy can get lost in the details. Without a consistent direction, people may be doing many different things, but the efforts can fall short. So take a look at each of the business, functional, and regional strategies to see if they are aligned to the enterprise. Assess how aligned the organization is toward achieving the business goals. If the daily activities aren't aligned to what really matters, how will you get people back on track?

Review the strategies for the brands and products to see if the strategies align with the corporate strategy. Assess the interdependencies between the businesses, functions, and geographies to identify what needs to be addressed. What areas must be adjusted to get all parts of the organization aligned and moving in the right direction? Capture your observations and actions on paper. Use these ideas to engage others in next steps.

Walk through each of the major business elements and assess how well the organization is performing in each of them. Then look across all the elements to determine whether business efforts overall are complementing one another or warring with one another, and whether you find disconnects in the work activities. It helps to go back and forth from the enterprise view to the individual business, brand, functional, or regional views to determine key priorities. Look for what's working and where the business connections can be improved. Also review the strategic initiatives. These initiatives usually require cross-organizational collaboration. Often, you will find disconnects and difficulties in carrying out these initiatives. Where would better cross-organizational dialogue enhance these efforts?

Assess the Talent

Executing the strategy comes down to the people, processes, and systems that are in place to enable the work to get done. Processes and systems are, of course, created and executed by people, not machines. You have had a chance to meet many of your people. From your vantage point, does the organization have the right talent and capability to follow through on its business plans? Where are the leadership strengths in the organization? What developmental needs are required to enhance capability? Formulate your ideas, so you can put in place a talent strategy that aligns with the overall strategic direction. Make sure to also take a look at the rewards and compensation programs to determine if they are aligned with the business metrics. People may be doing the wrong things when the rewards systems are out of sync with the business metrics.

Consider enlisting the Human Resources leader to assist in crafting a clear picture of the talent plan. Also, utilize the managers throughout the business and tap into their insights on talents and capabilities in their units.

Execute Business Strategy

Most incoming executives will make changes. Many strategic initiatives, however, fall short because of poor execution. Great strategies and programs badly or insufficiently executed lead to missed goals. An entire shelf of books could be dedicated to addressing strategies to deploy changes. This brief section is meant to get you thinking about the changes you will be making and the impact they will have on the people you are counting on to support those changes.

It's easy to pull the trigger on a change before the implications have been fully explored. So you will want to spend as much time leading the changes as you did coming up with the strategic concepts themselves. If you understand the organization's history and approach to deploying initiatives, the insights you glean will provide clues about the actions you will need to take to make leading initiatives more effective.

In your assessment of the business, how well does the organization deploy and execute strategies, processes, and programs? What project and change management tools are available to implement the solutions? As it pertains to executing change, what does the organization do well, and what could be enhanced? How are your fellow leaders engaged in leading change? What will it take to get the organization to being "implementation-savvy"?

Assess whether you need to adjust current initiatives or deploy new ones. In your assessment, determine how you will lead the current initiatives that you are inheriting.

Before you embark on making changes to the business, answer the following questions in detail:

◆ What is your vision of the future?
◆ How will these changes positively affect customers, revenues, and earnings?
◆ Why is it important to make these changes now?
◆ How prepared is the organization to take on the changes you are proposing?
◆ Where do you expect the leaders and others to resist the changes?
◆ How does the organization currently implement change? Are additional tools and methodologies at hand that could help with implementation? Do these have a track record of being effective in implementing change?
◆ How will you prepare your senior management team to get aligned around the changes?
◆ What is your overall plan to achieve the desired outcomes?

The table in Figure 23-1, Observations and Key Themes, provides a way to capture the findings and observations you collected during your transition and to prioritize the actions going forward. This will let you chart the business direction, cultivate the talent, and execute the business strategy to achieve the business outcomes.

Observations and Key Themes

Figure 23-1

Observations & Key Themes	Risks	Ways to Mitigate Risks	Recommended Action

Chapter 24

Sharing Your Observations

The secret of leadership is simple: Do what you believe in.
Paint a picture of the future. Go there. People will follow.

— Seth Godin

People will want to hear your opinions. You are in a unique position, because you have looked at all aspects of the business from an objective, "outsider" perspective. You are now able to see what's working and what's not. People will also be curious about how you plan to lead the organization and whether you will change the company's strategy, processes, and people. They will expect you to make some changes. They aren't quite sure, though, to what degree these changes will affect them. The fourth step in the Executive Transition Playbook (see Figure 2-1) is about Sharing the Information and insights you gained from looking at the business.

I suggest creating a presentation or report that allows you to outline key areas and themes to share your observations coherently and concisely. You will find that doing so will achieve the following:

- Help you discuss your plans with your boss, peers, and direct reports
- Enable you to align with others
- Give you a way to consistently and regularly update others on your plans

Craft Your Messages

Whenever you share your observations, that's a good time to demonstrate that you are taking full accountability for the business. Review the information you gathered and the insights from the exercises in Chapter 23 and the findings you identified in Figure 23-1 to prepare to share the information with the organization. Figure 24-1 suggests a presentation outline, which you can use or adapt to communicate your observations and insights effectively. By collecting your observations into key themes, it will be easier to share your ideas in both conversations and group forums. Consider what your audience needs to hear from you and the tone of your messages. Using the presentation as a guide, outline core themes and areas for action. It can be helpful to weave a story of the "who, what, when, where, and how:"

- What is the vision for the future? (Share your observations about the current state of the business. Then project what the future might look like.)
- Why is it important to make these changes?
- Who will be involved in the change?
- What processes will be used?
- How will success be measured?
- How will changes be deployed?
- What do you need from others to gain their buy-in and commitment?
- When do we need to hit certain milestones?

In essence, now that you have a sense of the business history and current situation, you will be working collaboratively with others to take the business into the future. Be sure your comments are in the spirit of helping, engaging, and enrolling others. Use language and examples that coach others toward a new way. Avoid terms that tend to disenfranchise the group, such as words that find fault with the current state of business or with former leaders. Instead, communicate a compelling case for change. This means less criticizing and more enrolling to create agreement, commitment, and buy-in to the solutions. It may be helpful to show how prior events built a solid foundation to prepare the organization for the next phase of the business. There may be market or other environmental factors that influence the decision to make significant changes now.

Some leaders use the presentation as an outline for a Leadership Summit to review the business strategies and plans going forward. They create collaborative work sessions to gain leadership alignment with the executive team. Depending on your business, you might engage the top 25, 50, or even 100 leaders in the solutions.

An Example of a Presentation Outline

Figure 24-1

1. **My thoughts and observations to date**
   - What I am excited about
   - What I have learned about the company's history
   - My observations, findings, and key themes so far
   - Questions I would like to cover

2. **Looking ahead**
   - Review the business targets
   - Share recommended actions, including a high-level timeline
   - Gain leadership alignment

3. **Working together**
   - Assemble the executive team
   - Set mutual expectations
   - Determine effective management processes
   - Develop a business calendar
   - Define our leadership actions

4. **Actions and next steps**

5. **Communications**
   - What do we need to share with others?

Your actions and involvement send a strong message that you are fully in charge and ready to take on the business challenges with the team. Use the newly identified themes as a springboard to initiate dialogues and discussions. Make sure that everyone becomes a real part of the solution. Some leaders start this process by working in smaller teams to flesh out ideas before sharing the direction with a broader audience. The method mostly depends on your business situation and your personal approach. The key aspect of this step is to share your findings and engage a broad audience in helping you carry out the next steps. This signals the end of your learning period.

As you complete this step of the Executive Transition Playbook, you will want to communicate any management process changes, re-confirm the business calendar, and set expectations and team guide-lines. The presentation outline in Figure 24-1 provides a section to discuss go-forward plans. In addition to the presentation, consider establishing a Communication Plan similar to the Transition Communication Plan described in Chapter 13. A Communication Plan will provide a structure and cadence to communicate key messages and keep others informed. Similarly, while you are sharing your findings, start incorporating any new leadership behaviors you have identified as desirable (see Figure 7-2).

Chapter 25

Stepping into Action: Beyond the Transition

The quicker you let go of old cheese, the sooner you find new cheese.

– Spencer Johnson

After about three to four months, your transition as the new leader customarily comes to an end. Then it will be time for you to demonstrate your value, contribute significantly to the organization, and achieve measurable results. The first few months in the new role have given you the opportunity to build credibility. But it is what you do over the next 6 to 18 months that determines your long-term success. The end of your transition is merely the beginning of your leadership. This is what you should be looking forward to: a time when you can truly start to serve and make a lasting contribution to the business.

If you have worked through the first four steps of the Executive Transition Playbook (see Figure 2-1), you now will have a better picture of how to enhance the business. This could involve clarifying the current strategy or developing a new one. Perhaps the executive team is not working well together, or it lacks the capability to effectively execute the strategy. Or you find that certain processes require updating to align with the strategy. Regardless of the specific issues you face, the next phase requires you to build an effective plan, communicate that plan to your stakeholders, and enroll others in the actions.

The fifth and final step of the Executive Transition Playbook is to Step into Action, which is an opportunity to create a What's Next

Plan. The What's Next Plan is a useful tool to map out how you wish to both take on the full business accountabilities and incorporate the changes you see need to happen. This plan takes the core themes you identified and maps those themes out over the next 18 months.

As part of the final phase of the transition, I work with leaders to chart their course for at least the next six months. Leaders can learn from professional athletes (among others) who regularly create goals and strategies to approach both training and competitive events. The strategic details of a plan allow the athletes to focus on executing the right strategies to compete at a world-class level. A What's Next Plan achieves the same purpose, of taking a leader from the transition period into the business cycle.

If you followed the Executive Transition Playbook, you learned about the organization, thought about the changes you will make, and identified and prioritized actions. You have worked on building your team, so that you can enroll others. You have carefully pondered your leadership style and actions, and you understand what is needed to lead this organization. Your What's Next Plan can capture all this information, giving you a clear and concise blueprint for what you will do going forward. As you share this plan with others, they will learn what they have to do to get engaged in your plans and follow your lead.

Many aspects of your Executive Transition Playbook can be repurposed to create your What's Next Plan. As you create this plan, focus on these areas:

Direction

Gain clarity on the direction, to ensure that the appropriate vision, strategy, and structure are in place.

Leadership Alignment

Check that the executive team is aligned and committed to moving in the same direction. Too frequently, great ideas fail because executives across the organization have conflicting ideas about and plans for where the business is headed.

Business Alignment

Review all the business elements to determine that each is suitably aligned with the business strategy. Processes and organizational structure should support the overall strategy, yet they can take on lives of their own or even be modified when people find it difficult to carry out the process as designed. Worse yet, many processes aren't documented, so different people may perform the process in different ways.

Role Clarity

Clearly define your business role, and help others define their own roles. Great strategies stall when people are unclear about what they are supposed to do. When smart people are not clear about their roles, they can create their own definitions, which may be off the mark. It is a waste of time, effort, and money for a star performer to do work that does not positively contribute to your strategy. So work with the executive team to identify the key leadership behaviors needed, especially if some of the activities are new or may be resisted.

Call to Action

Prepare the organization for the business changes. Bring people to action through timely, compelling messages that cascade throughout the organization. Be sure to include in your plan the actions needed to change both processes and behaviors, so that people can carry out the strategic direction.

Calendaring Your Milestones and Events

Develop an organizational business calendar to sequence and match the events to the kind of interactions and activities that will enable the work to be accomplished. You may have inherited a company business calendar; if such a calendar does not exist, create one. Your transition is a good opportunity to make any adjustments to fit the new direction.

Engagement

Continue to cultivate relationships. Build on the solid relationships you developed in the first three months, and continue to earn people's trust and respect over time. Doing so takes consistency in how you interact, communicate, and lead. Be sure to reach out to a broad cross section of people, so that you can learn how well your implementation efforts and leadership are working.

What's Next Plan Timeline				Figure 25-1
30 Days	**60 Days**	**90 Days**	**120 Days**	**180 Days**

Communications

Update your leadership communications strategy to match the needs of the business, going forward. Most leaders do not communicate enough. They get busy solving problems and forget to keep people informed. You can stay in touch by creating a plan for regular communication. Identify key touch points on which to solicit feedback, then learn about what is working (or not) in the organization. Use these touch points to coach others, remove obstacles, and resolve issues.

The What's Next Plan helps to keep the strong momentum and cadence of staying connected for months to come. You will be able to move from the "honeymoon" period to consistently effective daily operations in a smooth, seamless manner. Consider mapping the activities across a timeline such as the What's Next Plan Timeline depicted in Figure 25-1.

Use the What's Next Plan to get others involved in the actions going forward. The key is to create a narrative that enables you and others to capitalize on the ideas and insights you collected during the transition period. Pulling the information together into a What's Next Plan helps to move the ideas to action. This final exercise generates a firm foundation from which you can lead the organization over the next year, and for years to come.

Chapter 26

Final Thoughts

In today's highly competitive environment, leaders are growing businesses and are establishing and expanding healthy organizations through the actions of many individuals. Like them, you must consider how you will choose the best ways to serve the business you have been asked to lead. Your objective is to find the quickest path to gaining knowledge and traction in this role, so that you can add value to the efforts of others. You will need to pay close attention to what others require to do their jobs effectively, and as their leader you will have to provide a safe environment for people to interact, share a diversity of ideas, and come to agreement on the best path forward.

My hope is that an Executive Transition Playbook provides a strategic and operational approach to managing your transition. I trust that your Playbook resonates well with you and inspires you to spend this short transition period wisely. Further, I encourage you to use all the information in this book, modifying the Playbook and the other ideas to fit your business situation. My goal for the book has been to help you work through your strategy, plan your approach, and act in such a way that you can be of highest service to others in the organization.

An important point I want to restate is the importance of taking care of yourself first. Only then can you develop your leadership approach and create the balance to have the capacity, focus, and energy to engage others. A small amount of time spent on correct planning can go a long way in preparing you to show up well in the many venues of your business and your personal life, combined. You will then be prepared to assist others. When you employ a plan such as the Executive Transition Playbook, your intentions will begin to match your actions, and your actions will surely have a positive impact on the work of others.

When you are clear on a direction, you have a foundation from which to pivot and make changes as needed. If the foundation isn't strong, you may find yourself overly engrossed in many activities and moving in numerous directions; however, you may see minimal results, and the people around you may struggle to follow your lead.

It has been a privilege for me to share with you ways to elevate your leadership during the transition into a new role. While the concepts I lay out in this book make common sense, it requires effort on your part to make them your own. It is one thing to understand a concept, but it's truly another to put it into practice. The easiest things can get overlooked as being thought "too simple," even though these items may be the very underpinnings of more-complex activities.

Your Executive Transition Playbook provides ample tools for your journey into your new role. Many of my colleagues find these tools useful in handling other business changes, as well. You will do yourself and your colleagues a favor by using the proven tools I have outlined in this book to move along the path to high-performing leadership. You will be setting yourself — and others — up for success.

I will leave you with this final thought as you step into the new role:

> *Anyone can make the simple, complicated. It takes an extraordinary leader to take complex and complicated issues and make them simple.*
> – Adapted from jazz great Charles Mingus

As you work with others, strive to find the simplicity and clarity of solutions that will engage and inspire others.

I would welcome hearing about your leadership successes and challenges as you navigate the changing business environment. To send a note, and for more information, visit **www.executivetransitionplaybook.com**.

My best wishes to you, as you continue serving others through your thoughtful leadership.

Suggested Reading

Ken Blanchard and Spencer Johnson, *The New One Minute Manager* (New York: HarperCollins Publishers, 2015)

The authors have updated their 1980s classic, which continues to be a great reminder of fundamental principles for leaders and their important roles in serving organizations.

Larry Bossidy and Ram Charan, *Execution: The Discipline of Getting Things Done* (New York: Crown Business, 2002)

The authors share a no-nonsense approach to achieving results, using a simple model focused on strategy, process, and people. They provide insights to lead any business.

William Bridges, *Transitions: Making Sense of Life's Changes* (Boston: Da Capo Press, 2004)

The author outlines ways to navigate the psychological impacts of transitions in a way that honors the ending, a neutral zone, and a new beginning. He created a body of knowledge to help individuals and organizations navigate change. The exercises he presents help guide the reader through personal exploration of transitions. *Managing Transitions*, another book by the same author, focuses on how to assist others in business transitions.

Michael Carroll, *Awake at Work: 35 Practical Buddhist Principles for Discovering Clarity and Balance in the Midst of Work's Chaos* (Boston: Shambhala Publications, 2004)

The author shares Buddhist wisdom to turn business issues into opportunities. He uses ancient Eastern principles to inspire the reader to look at work as energizing and fulfilling.

Ram Charan, Stephen Drotter, and James Noel, *The Leadership Pipeline: How to Build the Leadership Powered Company* (San Francisco: John Wiley & Sons, 2011)

The authors offer a structure and insights on issues that leaders face as they move up the career ladder. The book contains many insights into traps and tips for successfully moving from the role of an individual contributor to that of a group business executive.

Stephen R. Covey, *The 7 Habits of Highly Effective People: Powerful Lessons in Personal Change* (New York: Simon & Schuster, 1990)

This book is a classic read for anyone who wants to be inspired and transformed in their personal and business lives.

Aubrey Daniels, *Bringing Out the Best in People* (New York: McGraw-Hill, 2000)

The author is a master at outlining the role that leadership behavior plays in getting results. His book is a short course on the ins and outs of applied behavioral science. Many leaders may be aware of the concepts, but what gets them into trouble can be the lack of follow-through. The author puts these ideas in the context of the business world.

Peter F. Drucker, Frances Hesselbein, and Joan Snyder Kuhl, *Peter Drucker's Five Most Important Questions: Enduring Wisdom for Today's Leaders* (Hoboken, NJ: John Wiley & Sons, 2015)

Drucker's questions are timeless and continue to be relevant in today's business world. This short, easy-to-read book should be a constant companion for any leader wanting to make a difference.

Seth Godin, *Tribes: We Need You to Lead Us* (New York: Penguin Group, 2008)

This book is a quick read about the power of bringing people together to solve problems. It will inspire you to find the collective power in your own organization.

Dan Harris, *10% Happier: How I Tamed the Voice in My Head, Reduced Stress without Losing My Edge, and Found Self-Help That Actually Works—A True Story* (New York: HarperCollins, 2014)

The author shares his journey into mindfulness meditation and other ancient Eastern practices. He tells how these practices helped him find a healthy balance in his high-powered career.

Gay Hendricks, *The Big Leap: Conquer Your Hidden Fear and Take Life to the Next Level* (New York: HarperCollins, 2009)

We all have "fears," a word that isn't always accepted in business conversation, which is an unfortunate omission. The author demonstrates how to eliminate the barriers to success by overcoming false fears and beliefs.

Phil Jackson with Hugh Delehanty, *Eleven Rings: The Soul of Success* (New York: Penguin Books, 2013)

Sports writers call basketball coach Jackson the "Zen Master" because he inspired his players to look past the fame and fortune and to consciously play the game they love. For leaders looking for practical ways to incorporate mindfulness into their own leadership practices, Jackson shares insightful stories of how he used these concepts to lead two professional teams to NBA titles.

Nancy Kline, *More Time to Think: A Way of Being in the World* (London: Cassell, 2009)

The author has been studying and writing books on the topic of thinking for decades. She provides perspectives on how to help yourself, and others, find the space to think. In this hectic world where people want things done "yesterday," she shares why we may be getting in our own way.

Patrick Lencioni, ***The Five Temptations of a CEO: A Leadership Fable*** (San Francisco: Jossey-Bass, 1998)

This is a wonderful tale of a CEO who knew he was failing. It depicts the few simple behaviors that any leader should consider practicing.

Jim Loehr and Tony Schwartz, ***The Power of Full Engagement: Managing Energy, Not Time, Is the Key to High Performance and Personal Reward*** (New York: Free Press, 2003)

If you are looking for an overall balance of your life and leadership, the authors can help you. They outline a simple model and set of tools to balance your physical, mental, emotional, and spiritual selves to be able to perform at your very best.

Michelle and Dennis Reina, ***Trust and Betrayal in the Workplace: Building Effective Relationships in Your Organization*** (Oakland, CA: Berrett-Koehler, 2015)

The authors masterfully share decades of research and work with corporate clients to help their readers understand how to build trust and support high-performing organizations. Don't be scared off by the title. The writers have a very practical model to help leaders enhance their own personal awareness and gain a perspective on what others may be experiencing as they build "trusting" organizations.

Robin Sharma, ***The Monk Who Sold His Ferrari: A Fable about Fulfilling Your Dreams and Reaching Your Destiny*** (New York: Free Press, 2011)

The author is a great storyteller who weaves leadership principles into his fabled stories. The messages are simple and inspiring.

Simon Sinek, *Start with Why: How Great Leaders Inspire Everyone to Take Action* (London: Penguin Group, 2009)

The author is all about finding an organization's, or an individual's, life purpose. This book is all about the "why." The author also has delivered a stimulating TED Talk that highlights the reason for you to find your "why."

Shunryu Suzuki, *Zen Mind, Beginner's Mind* (Boston: Shambhala Publications, 2011)

This spiritual classic is a must-read for anyone looking to find quiet and stillness through meditation and mindfulness. Every time you read it, new insights reveal themselves.

Julian Treasure, "5 Ways to Listen Better," TED Talk, July 2011
www.ted.com/talks/julian_treasure_5_ways_to_listen_better

Many executives are told they need to work on their listening skills, but few are shown how to practice listening. This TED Talk captures the essence of why we struggle to listen. This is a captivating speaker with amazing insights. He shares a compelling reason why a few minutes of sitting in silence (some call it meditation) really works.

Acknowledgments

This book would not have been possible without the insights and support of many people. I am deeply grateful for the extraordinary leaders I come in contact with every day.

First and foremost, I will be forever grateful to my family, especially my darling husband, Michael House, who has been my sounding board and so indispensable in helping me keep things logical and simple; thank you for your love, understanding, and encouragement through every iteration. Thanks also to my favorite guys, my sons Garrett and Evan House; I learn something from you every day, with your thoughtful questions and ideas. The world is a better place because you are in it. I hope this book provides both of you insights as you enter the business world.

Thank you to my sister, Jessica Payne, for providing me the Los Angeles book retreats to write the manuscript as well as the much-needed dinner breaks. Thanks also to the many leaders who have used these concepts to create their individualized Executive Transition Playbooks as they entered new jobs. Each leader sheds new learnings and reminds me of the importance of a well-defined set of goals, strategies, and plans that guides all great leaders. Your passion to make a difference to the companies and people you serve is inspiring!

In writing this book, I drew on the wisdom of countless leaders I have met over my decades in business. Many of them were willing to share their stories and even to work with the materials. I thank each and every one of you.

My deepest thanks to my colleagues and friends who read early drafts and offered sage advice. I am particularly grateful to Todd Lachman, Kristen Clendaniel Clark, Derrick Samuel, Linda Van

Valkenburgh, Bill Brimmer, Pam Magoon, Geoffrey Akiki, Orville Aarons, and Catherine Carlisi — for their reviews and thoughtful feedback, including their personal stories, terrific suggestions, and ideas that came out in our discussions. My gratitude goes to Robert Maher for brainstorming scenarios, working through the exercises, and reminding me on a regular basis to stay the course. Each of you truly enhanced the content. I hope you will recognize your contributions throughout the book.

And many thanks to my accountability partners, who are extraordinary executive coaches and authors: Jasbindar Singh and Stuart Elliott. Our weekly calls gave me the "mojo" to keep writing, from the first draft to the final version. Thanks for encouraging me to have the confidence to bring my authentic voice and holistic view to this important leadership topic.

I am profoundly grateful to my editor, Deirdre Silberstein of Silberstein & Associates, for her strategic insights and superb editing, for her guidance on how to lay out the book, and for her energy and enthusiasm as she pored over every draft to help me bring the contents to life. Thank you to Lynn Amos, of Fyne Lyne Ventures, who created a simple, elegant cover and a layout of the book that make it easy for readers to use the information. I truly appreciate the efforts of Patricia Bayer and Mark Woodworth in editing the manuscript, and of Patti Danos, whose energy and passion helped me find the right words, whether for the title or cover copy.

A special thanks also goes to Christy Tryhus, of Mission Marketing Mentors, who was indispensable with advice and coaching as I navigated through the writing process.

This book is dedicated to my mother, Judy Potts, and my late father, Daniel Potts, who always inspired me and encouraged me to dream big. I am eternally grateful for their guidance, for knowing when to show me the way, and for sensing when I needed the freedom to find it on my own.

I hope this book inspires you, my readers, to take steps to lead your transitions into new roles with energy and excellence, and with a passion to make the business better than when you took on your new role. By choosing this book, you have demonstrated courage to practice new leadership approaches and to serve the organizations that promoted you into the role. May you find the path to serve at your best!

About the Author

Hilary Potts has dedicated her career to helping others perform at their best. She advises some of the world's most prominent organizations to successfully transform the way businesses and leaders work. She works closely with executives to create solutions that fit both the business and the leadership.

Whether she is working with an executive one-on-one or engaging the management team, she focuses on how to bring out the best in people during times of change. With her guidance, leaders get clear on the direction, and people work together to make better decisions and execute plans more efficiently. Through teamwork, building trust, and constancy of purpose, leaders can go beyond what they thought possible.

Hilary Potts is no stranger to leading and transforming businesses. Before founding The HAP Group, she served as CEO and President of CLG, a global leader of performance-based consulting. She spent the first 15 years of her career at Union Carbide, a Fortune 500 company, where she held a variety of sales and business management positions. Hilary earned her BS and MS in chemical engineering from Clarkson University.

Hilary lives in Middlebury, Connecticut, with her husband, Michael House, and two sons, Garrett and Evan.

To learn more about how Hilary works with clients, please visit **www.HilaryPotts.com**. For additional information and resources go to **www.executivetransitionsplaybook.com**.

Working with the Author

Hilary Potts and Her Team Can Help You Lead Your Next Change

If you would like more information about how Hilary Potts and her team can help you or your organization, visit **www.HilaryPotts.com**. There you will find valuable information, such as:

- The Executive Transition Playbook Program, including resources, ideas, programs, and workshops to aid leaders transitioning into a new role

- The Executive Transition Assessment – a self-assessment tool aimed to help incoming leaders identify and diagnose ways to make the most of the first few months in a new position

- Details on how you can book Hilary and her team for consultations, speaking events, coaching engagements, or workshop programs

Hilary and her team at The HAP Group are devoted to guiding individuals and organizations to effectively lead and navigate change, whether at the individual or enterprise level. The HAP Group partners with leaders and organizations to provide solutions that fit the situation, so as to achieve the intended business outcomes.

If you wish to connect with Hilary and her team directly, send an email to **www.info@hapgrp.com** and someone will contact you.

Made in the USA
Middletown, DE
01 October 2016